The Unashamed

Sharing the Word

The Unashamed
Learning the Inductive Method
of Bible Study

Clay A. Kahler

Foreword by
Philip Popejoy, Ph.D.

WIPF & STOCK · Eugene, Oregon

THE UNASHAMED
Learning the Inductive Method of Bible Study

Copyright © 2011 Clay A. Kahler. All rights reserved. Except for brief quotations in critical publications or reviews, no part of this book may be reproduced in any manner without prior written permission from the publisher. Write: Permissions, Wipf and Stock Publishers, 199 W. 8th Ave., Eugene, OR 97401.

Wipf & Stock
An imprint of Wipf and Stock Publishers
199 W. 8th Avenue, Suite 3
Eugene OR, 97401
www.wipfandstock.com

ISBN 13: 978-1-61097-612-1

Manufactured in the U.S.A.

ACKNOWLEDGEMENTS

There are many people who I need to thank for their assistance in the production this book. First, to my many seminary professors who taught me well. These theologians not only taught me to study the Bible and Theology, but more importantly they taught me to think. I also want to thank the staff and students of the Midwest College of Biblical Studies, especially the students of the 2011 Inductive Bible Study Methods Course.

Then I owe the members and leaders of the First Baptist Church of Orrick MO. for their patience and their love. It is a privilege to serve as your pastor and I hope to continue until the Lord comes back.

Finally I want to thank Dr. Phil Popejoy for his proofreading of this manuscript, and willingness to confront my many mistakes. His efforts made this volume possible.

FOREWORD

Dr. Clay Kahler is a pastor, educator, and friend. He loves reading, studying and sharing the Word of God. *The Unashamed: Learning the Inductive Method of Bible Study* is an example of Clay's desire to share the Gospel. In *The Unashamed*, Clay shares with the reader Paul's letter to Philemon in scholarly detail by using the inductive method of study.

Inductive logic is a specific type of reasoning. It involves moving the individual from a set of specific facts to a general statement or conclusion. Paul's letter to Philemon may be his shortest letter recorded in Scripture but it is also an incredibly important text. By using the inductive Bible study method, Clay provides the reader with a Bible-based tool to study Philemon by observing the facts, investigating Paul's motives and reasons behind his letter and then offering life applications relevant to reader's life experiences.

The Unashamed is not a casual read. Begin with prayer before starting the study. The reader needs to set aside uninterrupted time to read and then utilize this text. Answer the questions at the end of each section.

The Unashamed uses the three essential steps of Inductive Bible studies: observation, interpretation and application. Observation is necessary in inductive Bible studies because it provides understanding to the passages context.

Observation only goes so far. The reader must also seek out the letter's interpretation and then apply what has been learned. Interpretation means to explain or tell the meaning of something and the presenting information in understandable terms. A synonym for interpretation is hermeneutics. The related Greek verb hermeneuo means to bring understanding of what is conveyed in another language, making it clear and intelligible.

Finally, the reader must apply what he or she has learned. Inductive Bible study, in fact, is not complete, unless you have an application. Bible study without application is like ―Faith without works!"

The inductive method of study is a skill that must be learned. If you are ready to enrich your Bible study by learning the inductive method of study, I strongly recommend Dr, Clay Kahler's, *The Unashamed: Learning the Inductive Method of Bible Study* .

Dr. Philip Popejoy
Richmond, Missouri

Table of Contents

- PREFACE 9
- CHAPTER 1 THE VALUE OF BIBLE STUDY 11
  - The Value of Study for Personal Living 11
  - The Value of Study for Personal Sanctification 15
  - The Enablement for Personal Bible Study 19
  - The Value of Study Tools 22
  - Inductive vs. Deductive Bible Study 29
  - Preserving the fruit of Personal Bible Study 32
- CHAPTER 2 THE SKILL OF OBSERVATION 35
  - Bible Reading 40
  - Paraphrasing 48
  - The Student, the Fish, and Agassiz 54
  - Learning to Observe 61
- CHAPTER 3 SKILL OF INTERPRETATION 69
  - Principles of Interpretation 73
  - Perspective 79
  - Literal Interpretation 80
  - Discovering the Theme of the Book 86
  - Paragraph Re-Titling 88
  - Evaluation 91
  - Charting a Bible Book 92
  - Syntactical Analysis 94
  - Introducing Key Connecting Words 96
  - The Rhetorical Method 110
  - Figures of Speech 116
  - Historical Interpretation 121
  - Author / Recipient Study 123
  - Cultural Study 131
  - Geographical Study 134
  - Historical Study 136
  - Grammatical Analysis 140
- CHAPTER 4 THE SKILL OF CORRELATION 169
  - The Biographical Method 170
  - Word Studies 171
  - Conclusion 179
- CHAPTER 5 APPLICATION 181
- CHAPTER 6 WRAP UP 189
- BIBLIOLOGY 195

Be diligent to present yourself approved to God, a worker who does not need to be ashamed, rightly dividing the word of truth.
-2 Timothy 2:15

PREFACE

Most believers depend on the ministry of a pastor, teacher or other Christian leader to interpret and apply Scripture for them. It is God's intention that every believer be able to interpret for themselves (2 Tim 2:15). It is the duty of the pastor-teachers to equip the saints for the work of the ministry. This includes interpretation, application and study of God's Word.

That's what this book is all about. Throughout this study the student will learn the importance of rightly interpreting and rightly applying the truths they find. This book will teach you how to do that, using the book of Philemon as a laboratory.

We who speak English are blessed with an entire workshop of tools, which make Bible study more efficient. Just keeping up with the array of available tools is an awesome task. This study will help you discover those tools which best fit your spiritual goals and will teach you how to use them proficiently.

It is my prayer that you will become a thoroughly equipped believer, able to feed yourself the good nourishing food of God's Word, rightly applying it to your life to the end that you grow to spiritual maturity (Heb 5:12-14). God has placed the Holy Spirit within each and every true believer for this very purpose (John 16:13).

Enjoy the feast!

Clay A. Kahler, Ph.D.

Chapter One
THE VALUE OF BIBLE STUDY

Personal Bible Study is study in which an individual, guided by the Holy Spirit, studies the Scriptures for the purpose of personal enrichment and discovery.

The Value of Study for Personal Living.

> "Be diligent to present yourself approved to God, a worker who does not need to be ashamed, rightly dividing the word of truth."
> -2 Timothy 2:15

"Be diligent" is translated from the Greek word "spoudazo." It means to continue to exert effort in the face of opposition. This can mean physical opposition or the kind of mental opposition that comes from facing a seemingly overwhelming study task.

"Approved" translates the Greek word "dokimos" which means to put something to the test with the hope of finding it suitable for its intended purpose. At the end of an assembly line an inspector tests the finished product with the hope that is proves acceptable. If the believers are diligent, they too will be suitable for God's intended purpose.

"Unto God" reminds us that the inspector of our lives is not our pastor, our professor, our parents, or our friends, but God Himself. If God is pleased with us what man can lay a charge at our feet?

"A worker" explains to us that as believers we are to be working for God. Ephesians 2: 8-9 are key verses that declare that salvation is by faith alone, not by works. But Ephesians 2:10 balances this truth with the truth that we are saved **unto** good works, that is for the purpose of doing good works. All believers are to be workers for God.

"Who does not need to be ashamed" gives us another benefit of being diligent. If we are diligent we will not only be suitable for God's intended work for us, we will not be ashamed because we are fulfilling what God wants us to do in life.

"Rightly dividing the Word of truth" tells us the object of our diligence. It says literally that we are to "cut a straight line" through the Word of truth. I am reminded of a master carpenter who is cutting straight down a line. If his cut is straight, both pieces will be suitable for use. For this to happen he must leave the right amount of wood on each side of his cut. Likewise, when a believer interprets the Word of God he must leave just the right things on each side of the line between them.

> "All Scripture is given by inspiration of God, and is profitable for doctrine, for reproof, for correction, for instruction in righteousness, that the man of God may be complete, thoroughly equipped for every good work."
> -2 Timothy 3:16-17

"All Scripture" is literally "all the thing written." As one old country preacher put it once, "The Bible is God's Word, from the table of contents to the concordance.

"Is given by inspiration of God" is one word in Greek, "theopneustos." This word is a verbal adjective and carries the idea that the thing written is as much the Word of God as if it had been directly breathed (exhaled) out of God's mouth. Of course that is not how we got God's Word. Holy men of God spoke as they were borne along by the Holy Spirit (2 Peter 1:21b).

"And is profitable for doctrine, for reproof, for correction, for instruction in righteousness" directs our thoughts to the value of the inspired Word of God. Doctrine is teaching. Reproof is to inform of wrongdoing. Correction is assisting the reader to get back on the right track. Instruction refers to child-training. All of these activities are accomplished by a steady diet of God's Word and are accomplished in righteousness.

"That the man of God may be complete" gives us the purpose for God's Word. It is given so that the believer – not the unbeliever – may be properly outfitted with the tools necessary, that he or she may have everything needed to live a righteous and God honoring life. It must be said that without the Word of God, there is no supply.

"Thoroughly equipped for every good work" describes the extent of the outfitting. The Word of God is all that we need to do all of the works that God has assigned to us. From this verse we deduce the doctrine of *sola Scriptura (Scripture alone)*, saying that the Scriptures alone are our rule for faith and practice because they are sufficient to equip us to do all that God wants us to do.

NOTE: It is this doctrine, in part, that teaches us that there is no need for further or new revelation. God has, in His wisdom and love, given us everything necessary. The Word of God is complete and sufficient in and of itself.

The Value of Study for Personal Sanctification.

In His high-priestly prayer, the Lord Jesus Christ prayed for those who would become believers through the ministries of the men that He had trained and left here on earth. His prayer included this request:

> "Sanctify them by Your truth.
> Your Word is truth."
> -John 17:17

"Sanctify them by Your truth." To sanctify is to set apart for a special purpose. Jesus' request was that His modern day followers (that is you and me), like His early followers, would be set apart by the Father for a particular use. This setting apart would take place by means of God's truth.

"Your Word is truth." It is His word that God uses to set us apart, to remove us from worldliness and establish us in His will for His purpose (Eph 1:9). The Word of God is what makes the difference in the lives of the children of God. If we are to be sanctified, set apart for God's own purpose, we must be full of God's Word.

The Value of Study for Personal Ministry.

The study of God's Word equips us for Christian living and for personal sanctification. It also equips us for ministry.

> "...you also, as living stones, are being built up a spiritual house, a holy priesthood, to offer up spiritual sacrifices acceptable to God through Jesus Christ."
> -1 Peter 2:5

"You also, as living stones, are being built up a spiritual house." New Testament believers are being made into a temple for the Lord. This temple is not made with the lifeless stones that comprised the temples of the Old Testament, but is made of living stones, believers themselves.

"A holy priesthood." In the Old Testament only the male descendants of Aaron could be priests (Exodus 28:1). And only those who were in perfect physical condition could make the priestly offerings (Leviticus 21:21). In the New Testament all believers (male, female, health, sickly, Jew, Gentile) are made priests to God.

"To offer up spiritual sacrifices." The job description of the New Testament believer-priest is given: to offer up spiritual sacrifices. Unlike the Old Testament priests, who offered up blood sacrifices, the New Testament priest's sacrifices are spiritual, non- bloody sacrifices. This is because Jesus Christ put an end to the blood sacrifice by becoming the last physical sacrifice, on our behalf. By shedding His own blood He has put an end to the sacrificial system once and for all (Hebrews 9:12-15).

"Acceptable to God through Jesus Christ." The spiritual sacrifices we bring as believer-priests are acceptable to God because we offer them through our position in Jesus Christ. Just as we have access to God the Father through Jesus Christ (Ephesians 2:18) regardless of our background, our sacrifices are now acceptable to God the Father.

Only by "diligently" studying the Word of God will we discover what sacrifices God has instructed us to bring. By using the methods and tools that we will in this course, we will discover that the sacrifices are found in Romans 12:1 and Hebrews 13:15-16.

> "For by grace you have been saved through faith, and that not of yourselves; it is the gift of God, not of works, lest anyone should boast. For we are His workmanship, created in Christ Jesus for good works, which God prepared beforehand that we should walk in them."
> -Ephesians 2:8-10

"For by grace you have been saved through faith." It is by God's provision that we have received salvation, by means of our believing the good news of the Gospel: the death, burial, and resurrection of Jesus for our sins.

"And that not of yourselves, it is a gift of God." Even the faith to believe was not of our own strength;

it came as a gift of God. God gave me the faith to believe in the Gospel of His Son.

"Not of works, lest anyone should boast." Our salvation came through faith, not through anything that we said, or did. If we could earn our own salvation we would surely boast about it.

"For we are His workmanship, created in Christ Jesus for good works." We are God's masterpiece, his epic poem. He created us in Christ for the purpose of our doing good works. Notice that while the good works do not contribute in any way to our salvation, they are the normal result of salvation.

"Which God prepared beforehand, that we should walk in them." God has prepared some good works for each believer to do. Personal Bible study helps us to know what God wants us to do with our lives, our personal ministries.

> "As each one has received a gift, minister it to one another, as good stewards of the manifold grace of God."
> -1 Peter 4:10

"As each one has received a gift." Every believer has received a spiritual gift. A spiritual gift is a supernatural enabling of the believer by the Holy Spirit to perform a specific function in the Body of Christ with a degree of effectiveness that would otherwise not be possible.

"Minister it to one another." The purpose of having a spiritual gift is to allow each believer to minister to other believers. *This builds up the Body of Christ, the church.*

"As good stewards of the manifold grace of God." A steward was a servant who was highly trusted and managed the goods of the owner, very much like a general manager or financial planner today. Believers are to be good managers of the things that are entrusted to us by God, yet do not belong to us. This would include, but is not limited to, God's provision to meet the needs of others through the exercise of our spiritual gifts. This display of God's grace is called ―manifold" because it appears different in each believer.

So, we can see that personal Bible study is important for each believer's personal living, sanctification, and ministry. We must study the Word of God if we are to carry out these functions in a way that pleases God.

The Enablement for Personal Bible Study

The most important enablement that we possess for personal Bible Study is the teaching ministry of the Holy Spirit. In introducing the ministry of the Holy Spirit to his disciples, Jesus said:

> "But the Helper, the Holy Spirit, whom the Father will send in My name, He will teach you all things, and bring to your remembrance all things that I said to you."
> -John 14:26

"But the Helper, the Holy Spirit." Jesus refers to the Holy Spirit as the Helper. The Greek word is "paraklete," one called alongside to aide. God, the Holy Spirit indwells believers and acts as our constant companion and tutor.

"Whom the Father will send in My name." The Father sent the Holy Spirit in the name of the Lord Jesus Christ. Notice that all three persons of the Trinity are seen working together, on our behalf, in this verse.

"He will teach you all things." The Lord Jesus identifies teaching believers as a portion of the ministry of the Holy Spirit in the lives of believers.

"And bring to your remembrance all things that I said to you." The Holy Spirit also works in the lives of the children of God by bringing to remembrance the things that He has taught us. It is this ministry of the Holy Spirit that allows us to face persecution, temptation, and difficulty with confidence and strength.

> "However, when He, the Spirit of truth, has come, He will guide you into all truth; for He will not speak on His own authority, but whatever He hears He will speak; and He will tell you things to come."
> -John 16:13

"However, when He, the Spirit of Truth has come." The Holy Spirit is identified by Christ as the Spirit of Truth because He always ministers the truth. At the time the Lord was speaking the Holy Spirit was not yet indwelling believers as He is now.

"He will guide you into all truth," The Holy Spirit's function includes guiding believers so that they can discover the truth of God's word. The truth is found in the Scriptures (John 17:17), and the Holy Spirit is the agent guiding believers to find, understand, and apply it.

"He will not speak on His own authority, but whatever He hears He will speak." The Holy Spirit is not given the task of providing new revelation to believers, but taking that which the Father has formulated and guiding believers through it.

"And He will tell you things to come." Believers have always wanted to know what would happen next, and the disciples were no exception. They were especially concerned in light of the fact that Jesus had announced His imminent departure to heaven. The question on each of their lips was, —what will happen

then?" Jesus, made sure that these frightened, unsure men would know that they would not be left to fend for themselves, but that God, the Holy Spirit would come to indwell them, guild them, help them, and that He had all of the answers that they sought.

The Value of Study Tools

The next aspect of enablement for personal Bible study is the proper use of appropriate tools. A Bible study tool is a tool that assists you in the carrying out your personal Bible study. If you need to dig a hole in the ground you could do it with your bare hands, however the proper use of a backhoe makes the task much more efficient, and in many cases more precise. You still do the work, but your efficiency is improved by the proper use of the appropriate tool.

We have learned that **it is the responsibility of every believer to interpret Scripture** (2 Timothy 2:15). You cannot turn that responsibility over to someone else, but you can employ tools to help you to better do your job.

A Bible study tool is something that provides help and assistance to a believer but does not interpret the Scripture for him. When something interprets Scripture for you it has ceased to be a tool. You are no longer being diligent and are, in essence, taking credit for someone else's work.

In this course we will learn about a variety of Bible tools. We will learn where to find them and what they can or cannot do, then we will learn how to use them.

The best possible source for Bible study tools is in your own personal library. However, most students are not generally able to buy every Bible study tool. Since these tools will assist you over and over again it is recommended that the student begin investing in these tools as you are able.

WHERE CAN YOU FIND STUDY TOOLS?
(Check all that apply)

❏ My personal Library. I own _____ volumes.

❏ Seminary Library

❏ A friend's, pastor's, or teacher's library.

❏ The internet.

❏ A Bible bookstore near me.

❏ Other: _____.

BIBLE STUDY TOOLS EXERCISE

This Exercise is designed to assist you to locate resources that you can use in your personal Bible study. In the first part of the Exercise you will identify general resources. In the second part you will locate and identify specific Bible study tools.

1. My personal library. I have _____ books and _____ periodicals, and _____ items available in computer format (Bible programs, access to internet tools).

2. The personal libraries of others. I could use the libraries of :

3. Bible College or Seminary libraries. Specifically:

4. I have access to these local Bible bookstores:

Specific Resources
For each of the categories listed below, locate specific resources and identify them by title, author, publisher, price and, from where you could obtain the resource.

A. Bible Atlases (3)

B. Bible Dictionaries (3)

C. Concordances, English (2)

D. Concordances, Greek (1)

E. Greek Lexicon (1)

F. Greek Word Studies (2)

G. Bible Manners and Customs (3)

H. Figures of Speech (1)

I. English Dictionary (1)

J. English Grammar Handbook (1)

K. Greek Grammar (1)

L. Bible Encyclopedias (2)

M. Interlinear Greek-English New Testament (1)

N. Bible Computer Programs (2)

So far we have seen that the Holy Spirit and Bible study tools are two means of enablement by which the believer can do effective personal Bible Study. Now let us examine how to best utilize these enablements to maximize our personal Bible study. Let's consider Bible Study methods.

A Bible study method is an ordered list of procedures which guides the believer in personal Bible study so that he gets the information he needs from the Bible.

Some Bible study methods include:

- Reading
- Paraphrasing
- Observation
- Syntactical Analysis
- Paragraph Titling
- Analytical Charting
- Historical/Political
- Cultural
- Geographical
- Biographical
- Grammatical
- Rhetorical
- Figures of Speech
- Word Studies
- Theological
- Topical
- Devotional
- Comparative

You will learn most of these methods in the course.

INDUCTIVE VS. DEDUCTIVE BIBLE STUDY

There are two major approaches to Bible study, inductive study and deductive study. Both were used by Jesus Christ in His teaching and both have advantages and disadvantages.

How are these methods of study different?

> –Strictly speaking, induction and deduction are opposite methods. In induction, you first observe, then conclude. In deduction you begin with a general principal or conclusion then observe whether the conclusions are true.[1]"

In induction you begin with the little pieces of a puzzle, and no picture. You assemble each piece one at a time, in order to see the picture that they make. You do not begin with any preconception of what the completed picture will be.

In deductive study you begin with a theory, a belief, or a hypothesis. You then examine the pieces to see if they really do support your hypothesis. When the Apostle Paul preached to the Jews at Berea the Scripture says that these Jews searched the Scripture daily to see if what Paul said was true (Acts 17:10-11). Paul was presenting new truth, and these Jews wanted to know if it agreed with the Scriptures they

---

[1] Jensen, Irving. *Independent Bible Study*, 1991, Chicago: Moody Press, p38.

already had. This is an example of the deductive method.

One of the major advantages of the deductive method is that it saves time. Instead of "reinventing the wheel," the student begins with the teachings of another. The student then evaluates these teachings with individual pieces he has from the Bible in an attempt to validate or invalidate the teaching. This process is much faster than if the student were to discover all of the truth for himself or herself. This is why deductive teaching is generally employed in most churches and schools today. The teacher or preacher desires to communicate as much truth as possible in as little time as possible.

There are also some significant downsides to deductive teaching. The student who is less careful may accept the teaching without giving it vigilant evaluation from God's Word. It is easy for this to happen because some of what is taught is directly from the Bible, but other parts of what is taught may be the opinion or preconception of the individual preacher or teacher. It is often very difficult to tell these two apart.

Another shortcoming of the deductive method is that the student may never really gain "ownership" of the truth. He may give assent to what is taught, but is likely to forget it in after time.

Inductive study has the advantage of requiring the student to put together his own belief system. While this takes considerably longer than deductive study, it will stick with the student much longer because he or she had to discover it and put it together, one step at a time.

Some students make the mistake of equating inductive Bible study with ―serious Bible study." They have assumed that because they worked and studied on their own that their study was inductive. Whenever the teacher or leader suggests a theme for a book of the Bible the study has become deductive. The task of the student now becomes to examine and see if the proposed theme is accurate or not.

Pure inductive Bible study is study in which the teacher or leader provides no information to the student about the Biblical passage being studied. The teacher simply becomes a coach who helps the student to stay motivated and a referee who keeps the student on track with the methods, so that the student can study the Scripture for themselves.

The intent of this book is to teach you how to do inductive study. Upon successful completion, you will you will be able to approach any of the sixty six books of Scripture and apply the methods that you have learned to study that book. You will be forever free of the need to ―eat spiritual food off someone else's plate." You will be able to feed yourself, under the leadership of the Holy Spirit, directly from the Word of God.

NOTE: This process is simply a tool that will allow you to gain a deeper understanding of God's Word, it is not meant to replace formal training or formal worship and study, but rather to enhance it.

Preserving the Fruit of Personal Bible Study

A diligent Bible student spends time and effort to understand the Bible and rightly apply it. It is profitable to record the results of your personal study for future use.

Educational psychology tells us that we benefit from the process of taking notes. By engaging not only our sight and hearing but also our thinking and writing process we are inclined to remember more than if we simply listen to a lecture or read a book.

The Flow of this Study

This book will be divided into four major parts. These are **observation**, **interpretation**, **correlation**, and **application**. Each will be dealt with in its own chapter, and we will learn to use tools and methods appropriate to that aspect of the overall study process.

Observation focuses on noticing what is in the Biblical text. It answers the question, "What does it say?" We learn to look for certain things. An example may be a carpenter who enters a room and notices that the molding does not match up properly. This minor detail may escape the attention of everyone else in the room.

The second major part of personal Bible study is **interpretation**. Interpretation answers the question, "What does it mean?" We will deal with interpretation in chapter three, using the model of literal, historical, grammatical interpretation.

Next in line is **correlation**. Correlation is a study of what other passages of Scripture teach in relation to the topic being studied. Correlation is based on the principle that Scripture is the best interpreter of Scripture. This helps us fit Scriptures together.

The final part of personal Bible study is **application**. Application answers the question, "So what?" God did not give us His Word to swell our heads with knowledge but to change our lives. When we get to the application section we will learn how to apply the principles of Scripture to our personal lives.

So, are you ready? Let the adventure begin!

Chapter Two
THE SKILL OF OBSERVATION

Observation is the starting point for the right application of Scripture. Until the student sees what the Bible says, he or she cannot interpret it, correlate it, or apply it to their own life. Those whose observation skills are lacking or underdeveloped are subject to be led like sheep to the slaughter, to be led astray by those many wolves who are seeking to deceive and mislead.

The Bible declares that our faith is a revealed faith. In 1 Corinthians 2:9-10 we read:

> "But as it is written: "Eye has not seen, nor ear heard, Nor have entered into the heart of man The things which God has prepared for those who love Him." But God has revealed them to us through His Spirit. For the Spirit searches all things, yes, the deep things of God."

This revelation was written down so that it could be accurately preserved through the centuries. God, in His wisdom has chosen to give us His Word in sixty six books, written in concert by His Holy Spirit and men. These human beings are called the ―human authors" of Scripture.

Each of these ―human authors" wrote using their own vocabulary and style. It is not surprising to find that Luke frequently used medical terminology because Luke was a physician. Likewise, it is not surprising to discover that Peter and John wrote like fishermen. Paul, the ―human author" of many of the New Testament books, wrote like a lawyer. As a Pharisee, Paul was a religious lawyer.

However, the ―human authors" were not alone in the process of inscripturation. Each book of the Bible also had a Divine Author, the Holy Spirit. This is explained in 2 Peter 1:21:

> "...for prophecy never came by the will of man, but holy men of God spoke as they were moved by the Holy Spirit."

For prophecy never came by the will of man. Prophecy was receiving revelation from God and speaking it out. This did not happen because man wanted it to happen. Prophecy was arranged by God, Himself.

But holy men of God spoke as they were moved by the Holy Spirit. When holy men of God received revelation from God and spoke it, they were under the direction of the Holy Spirit. The word "moved" means to be driven along and is used in Acts 27:15 of a ship in a storm, driven along by the wind. In a similar way the human authors of Scripture were driven along by the Divine Author, the Holy Spirit.

This process is called the "*dual authorship*" of Scripture. Each Bible book had a human author who was driven along by the Divine Author. So even though the human authors used their individual vocabularies and styles, they were never really in charge. God, the Holy Spirit superintended the process.

Understanding the process of getting the Word from God to us gives us confidence in His Word. But God didn't stop there. He explained to us the exact nature of the written Word.

> "All Scripture is given by inspiration of God, and is profitable for doctrine, for reproof, for correction, for instruction in righteousness..."
> 2 Timothy 3:16

All Scripture is given by inspiration of God. All Scripture is literally, "all the thing written." It refers to the written Word of God, all of it. It assures us that the Word of God carries with it the quality of inspiration and the authority of God, Himself. The word for inspiration is literally the word, "God-breathed." The claim is that the written Scriptures have the same quality as if God had personally breathed them out of His mouth!

And is profitable for doctrine, for reproof, for correction, for instruction in righteousness. What has been written down has the quality of God-breathedness and therefore it is profitable. It is useful for teaching me the truth. It is useful for reproof, which is telling me when I am wrong. It is profitable for correction, which is helping me which is setting me back on the right path. It is useful for instruction, which literally means "child-training." Each of these four accomplishments of Scripture in the life of the believer is done "in righteousness."

The importance of observing the Bible is that we are observing the plan of God written in words so that we can understand it. If we want to know His will then we must observe what He has said. Because God has been so careful to record this revelation for us it is very important that we pay attention to it.

When a soldier in a foreign land receives a letter from his wife or girlfriend he reads it over and over again to notice every possible inference, every single detail. He does this because he loves the one who has sent the letter. We ought to feel the same way about what our Heavenly Father has written to us. If we do we will be motivated to notice every stroke on the page.

In this chapter we will learn three methods of study that will help us to observe God's message to us:

1. Bible reading will give us the big picture.
2. Paraphrasing will help us to thoroughly and mechanically examine every word on the page.
3. The observation chart will assist us to observe what God has written topic by topic, theme by theme.

BIBLE READING

The first method of observation is Bible reading. For many believers, reading is the first thing that we do in personal Bible study. Here are a few things that will make your reading more profitable.

Physical Conditions for Reading.

Three elements impact our reading in the physical realm. These are posture, distractions, and light. You may have noticed that you are more attentive (although less comfortable) when you are sitting upright in a chair. Generally, people learn more when they read with erect posture than when they are lying in bed or spread out in their favorite recliner.

Distractions are other physical factors that impede observation while reading. Distractions may include music, television, children playing, the telephone, and other occurrences that draw our attention away from the text that we are reading. The Bible student must learn to manage these distractions to maximize the benefits of Bible reading. Just having a quiet place to get away from the affairs of daily life and keeping distractions to a minimum will greatly benefit you in your search.

One factor that will quickly diminish the effectiveness of reading is insufficient light. For maximum benefit in reading, the room should be well lighted to prevent squinting and general eye fatigue.

Mental Conditions for Reading.

There are mental conditions that impact the effectiveness of our reading as well. Alertness, expectation, and discipline are factors that can make Bible reading a joy or a chore. In order to get the most from our Bible reading we should read when we are mentally alert (whatever time of day that might be).

Our motivation and enjoyment will be greatly enhanced if we read with expectation. If we are only reading in order to "fulfill" some perceived duty, reading soon becomes a matter of fulfilling a commitment rather than seeking God's will and guidance. If, on the other hand, we read expecting God to lead and teach us, we eagerly look forward to the opportunity to delve into His Word, and our profit from reading is greatly increased. We will be looking at some methods of reading that harness the energy of our expectations.

Discipline can be defined as doing that which we know is for our own good, even if we do not feel like it. There are many mornings that I DO NOT feel like exercising. I even spend a great deal of energy creatively fashioning excuses as to why I shouldn't. However, by discipline, I press on. Similarly, when we approach Bible study, we need to press on. One way of accomplishing this is by having a regular time and place for personal Bible study.

Spiritual Conditions for Reading.

Just as there are physical and mental conditions that affect our reading, there are also spiritual conditions that will help or hinder us. The most important of these is fellowship with the Father.

We have fellowship with the Father when we offer our lives to Him. We are to pay attention to those things which are above, not to the things of this world (Colossians 3:2). When we enjoy this fellowship with God the Father we are open to the leading and teaching of the Holy Spirit, who makes up for what is lacking in our character, making us more like Jesus (Ephesians 5:18; Galatians 5:22-24). John calls this "walking in the light" (1 John 1:6-7).

When believers are out of fellowship with God the Father, the Holy Spirit begins the grieving process and ceases teaching (Ephesians 4:30). This process gains the attention of the erring believer in order to direct him or her back to a right relationship with the Father. This grieving process supplants the Holy Spirit's teaching ministry, so that believers when they are out of fellowship are not able to learn all that God has for them.

The result of all this is that believers need to be spiritually minded rather than carnally minded in order to gain from the teaching ministry of the Holy Spirit. This is the most important spiritual condition for personal Bible Study.

One-Sitting Reading.

One of the most valuable kinds of Bible reading is "one-sitting" reading. One-sitting reading is when the student reads the Bible book in one sitting in order to gain an overview or "big picture" view of the text. This is, of course, simple for short books and much more difficult for longer books. Bus by reading the entire book at one sitting the student is introduced to the context, the setting and the overall theme.

Reading for Plot.

When we read for plot we concentrate on the story line, particularly the action of the book. This is especially helpful for historical books, i.e. the Gospels, Acts, and the Old Testament historical narratives.

Reading for Doctrine.

Another approach to reading a Bible book is to read for doctrine. In this approach the student looks for a specific area of doctrine. Following is a list of some of the major areas of Bible doctrine that you will want to identify as you read for doctrine:

Doctrine of	Theological Title	Areas of Study
Bible	Bibliology	The Word of God
Dispensations	Dispensationalism	Dispensations, Covenants, Ages
God	Theology Proper	Nature of God, Trinity
Father	Paterology	Person and Works of the Father
Christ	Christology	Person and Works of the Son
Holy Spirit	Pneumatology	Person and Works of the Holy Spirit
Angels	Angelology	Spirit beings, Angels, Demons, Satan

Man	Anthropology	Origin and nature of man
Sin	Hamartiology	Unrighteousness, Sin, Trespass, Transgression
Salvation	Soteriology	All aspects of salvation
Christian Life	Sanctification	Spiritual Maturity
Church	Ecclesiology	The Body of Christ (church)
Last Things	Eschatology	Future events, Biblical Prophecy

Reading Biographically.

You can read a Bible book looking for the various characters that are described in the book. A more in-depth approach to this kind of study is undertaken in the biographical method of Bible study.

Reading Thematically.

You can read any Bible book looking for what it says about a particular theme such as faith, obedience, grace, etc. By looking for this theme your reading will be more focused and you are more likely to notice what is said about the subject.

Limitations on Reading.

The student should be aware of several factors which limit comprehension in reading. The eye gate alone (taking in information through the eyes) is not as effective as an eye/ear combination. It is best to use multiple senses whenever possible for optimum comprehension. Reading with a pencil – taking notes – generally increases comprehension.

The faster one reads (during one-sitting reading) the higher the comprehension generally will be. Spaced hours (hours spread out between readings) are generally more effective than massed hours (hours all together) in reading.

BIBLE READING EXERCISE

Read the book of Philemon following the directions below:

1. Read Philemon at one sitting using the Authorized King James Version.

2. Read Philemon at one sitting using the New King James Version.

3. Read Philemon at one sitting using the New International Version.

4. Read Philemon at one sitting using the New American Standard Version.

5. Read Philemon at one sitting using the New Living Version.

6. Read Philemon at one sitting using the Amplified Bible.

7. Read Philemon at one sitting using the Message.

8. Read Philemon for plot. Use the translation of your choice and record your reading below.

9. Read Philemon for one area of doctrine. Use the translation of your choice and record your reading below.

10. Read Philemon biographically. Use the translation of your choice and record your reading below.

Which translation did you prefer?

Why did you pick this one?

Do you see any value in reading different translations?

What did you notice in your reading for plot? Describe the events of the book in a few words.

What area of doctrine did you pick for your doctrinal reading? What does Paul teach about this doctrine in the Epistle to Philemon?

Paraphrasing

One of the most useful tools for observation is paraphrasing. The word paraphrase comes from two Greek words. *Para* meaning alongside of and *Phrasso,* to block up [words], or a group of related words. To make a paraphrase is to write a group of related words alongside another group of related words.

The purpose of paraphrasing in personal Bible study is to force yourself to look intently at each word in the text. It is not intended to improve the translation, either by making it simpler or by making it more accurate. Paraphrasing is an exercise in observation, NOT in interpretation.

The process of paraphrasing is simple. Place the text to be paraphrased in the left hand column on a sheet of paper. Write your paraphrase in the right hand column using the following methods.

1. *Substitution*: Replace one word with another word. Example: Lord → Jesus

2. *Expansion*: Replace one or more words with a greater number of words. Example: Lord → Jesus Christ

3. *Reduction*: Replace several words with a lesser number of words. Example: The Lord our Savior → Jesus

4. *Inversion*: Change the word order. Example: The Lord, Jesus Christ → Christ Jesus, The Lord

The most desirable method is method 1, substitution. You should try to substitute for as many words as possible. Some substitutions will require that you handle the text a phrase at a time, and you will use methods two or three, expansion or reduction. The fourth method, inversion, is the least desirable of all since it requires the smallest amount of mental interaction with the text. Remember, this is a mechanical method designed to help you notice and interact with every word in the text.

Paraphrase Worksheet

1 Paul, a prisoner of Christ

Jesus, and Timothy our

brother, To Philemon our

beloved friend and fellow

laborer,

2 to the beloved Apphia,

Archippus our fellow soldier,

and to the church in your

house:

3 Grace to you and peace

from God our Father and the

Lord Jesus Christ.

4 I thank my God, making

mention of you always in my

prayers,

5 hearing of your love and faith which you have toward the Lord Jesus and toward all the saints,

6 that the sharing of your faith may become effective by the acknowledgment of every good thing which is in you in Christ Jesus.

7 For we have great joy and consolation in your love, because the hearts of the saints have been refreshed by you, brother.

8 Therefore, though I might be very bold in Christ to command you what is fitting,

9 yet for love's sake I rather appeal to you--being such a one as Paul, the aged, and now also a prisoner of Jesus

Christ—

10 I appeal to you for my son Onesimus, whom I have begotten while in my chains,

11 who once was unprofitable to you, but now is profitable to you and to me.

12 I am sending him back. You therefore receive him, that is, my own heart,

13 whom I wished to keep with me, that on your behalf he might minister to me in my chains for the gospel.

14 But without your consent I wanted to do nothing, that your good deed might not be by compulsion, as it were, but voluntary.

15 For perhaps he departed for a while for this purpose, that you might receive him

forever,

16 no longer as a slave but more than a slave--a beloved brother, especially to me but how much more to you, both in the flesh and in the Lord.

17 If then you count me as a partner, receive him as you would me.

18 But if he has wronged you or owes anything, put that on my account.

19 I, Paul, am writing with my own hand. I will repay--not to mention to you that you owe me even your own self besides.

20 Yes, brother, let me have joy from you in the Lord; refresh my heart in the Lord.

21 Having confidence in your obedience, I write to you,

knowing that you will do even more than I say.

22 But, meanwhile, also prepare a guest room for me, for I trust that through your prayers I shall be granted to you.

23 Epaphras, my fellow prisoner in Christ Jesus, greets you,

24 as do Mark, Aristarchus, Demas, Luke, my fellow laborers.

25 The grace of our Lord Jesus Christ be with your spirit. Amen.

THE STUDENT, THE FISH, AND AGASSIZ
by the Student, Samuel H. Scudder[2]

NOTE: The following is a classic account of the importance of first-hand observation, and careful, intense, focused study. It teaches lessons that apply to almost any discipline. Indeed, it is widely used in colleges and universities across the U.S. as a teaching tool in both the humanities and the sciences.

Its lessons certainly apply to studying the Bible. Too often students of the Bible rely on second-hand, derivative knowledge, acquired from pastors, teachers, parents, books about the Bible, or other secondary sources. While all of these have their place, there is no substitute, in the end, for one's own first-hand study and experience of the Scriptures, and for the joy of discovery.

It was more than fifteen years ago that I entered the laboratory of Professor Agassiz, and told him I had enrolled my name in the scientific school as a student of natural history. He asked me a few questions about my object in coming, my antecedents generally, the mode in which I afterwards proposed to use the knowledge I might acquire, and finally, whether I wished to study any special branch. To the latter I replied that while I wished to be well grounded in all departments of zoology, I purposed to devote myself specially to insects.

"When do you wish to begin?" he asked.

"Now," I replied.

---

[2] *American Poems* (3rd ed.; Boston: Houghton, Osgood & Co., 1879): pp. 450-54.

This seemed to please him, and with an energetic "Very well," he reached from a shelf a huge jar of specimens in yellow alcohol.

"Take this fish," he said, "and look at it; we call it a *Haemulon*; by and by I will ask what you have seen."

With that he left me, but in a moment returned with explicit instructions as to the care of the object entrusted to me.

"No man is fit to be a naturalist," said he, "who does not know how to take care of specimens."

I was to keep the fish before me in a tin tray, and occasionally moisten the surface with alcohol from the jar, always taking care to replace the stopper tightly. Those were not the days of ground glass stoppers, and elegantly shaped exhibition jars; all the old students will recall the huge, neckless glass bottles with their leaky, wax-besmeared corks, half-eaten by insects and begrimed with cellar dust. Entomology was a cleaner science than ichthyology, but the example of the professor who had unhesitatingly plunged to the bottom of the jar to produce the fish was infectious; and though this alcohol had "a very ancient and fish-like smell," I really dared not show any aversion within these sacred precincts, and treated the alcohol as though it were pure water. Still I was conscious of a passing feeling of disappointment, for gazing at a fish did not commend itself to an ardent entomologist. My friends at home, too, were annoyed, when they discovered that no amount of *eau de cologne* would drown the perfume which haunted me like a shadow.

In ten minutes I had seen all that could be seen in that fish, and started in search of the professor, who had, however, left the museum; and when I returned, after lingering over some of the odd animals stored in the upper apartment, my specimen was dry all over. I dashed the fluid over the fish as if to resuscitate it from a fainting-fit, and looked with anxiety for a return of a normal, sloppy appearance. This little excitement over, nothing was to be done but return to a steadfast gaze at my mute companion. Half an hour passed, an hour, another hour; the fish began to look loathsome. I turned it over and around; looked it in the face -- ghastly; from behind, beneath, above, sideways, at a three-quarters view -- just as ghastly. I was in despair; at an early hour, I concluded that lunch was necessary; so with infinite relief, the fish was carefully replaced in the jar, and for an hour I was free.

On my return, I learned that Professor Agassiz had been at the museum, but had gone and would not return for several hours. My fellow students were too busy to be disturbed by continued conversation. Slowly I drew forth that hideous fish, and with a feeling of desperation again looked at it. I might not use a magnifying glass; instruments of all kinds were interdicted. My two hands, my two eyes, and the fish; it seemed a most limited field. I pushed my fingers down its throat to see how sharp its teeth were. I began to count the scales in the different rows until I was convinced that that was nonsense. At last a happy thought struck me -- I would draw the fish; and now with surprise I began to discover new features in the creature. Just then the professor returned.

"That is right," said he, "a pencil is one of the best eyes. I am glad to notice, too, that you keep your specimen wet and your bottle corked."

With these encouraging words he added --

"Well, what is it like?"

He listened attentively to my brief rehearsal of the structure of parts whose names were still unknown to me; the fringed gill-arches and movable operculum; the pores of the head, fleshly lips, and lidless eyes; the lateral line, the spinous fin, and forked tail; the compressed and arched body. When I had finished, he waited as if expecting more, and then, with an air of disappointment:

"You have not looked very carefully; why," he continued, more earnestly, "you haven't seen one of the most conspicuous features of the animal, which is as plainly before your eyes as the fish itself. Look again; look again!" And he left me to my misery.

I was piqued; I was mortified. Still more of that wretched fish? But now I set myself to the task with a will, and discovered one new thing after another, until I saw how just the professor's criticism had been. The afternoon passed quickly, and when, towards its close, the professor inquired,

"Do you see it yet?"

"No," I replied. "I am certain I do not, but I see how little I saw before."

"That is next best," said he earnestly, "but I won't hear you now; put away your fish and go home; perhaps you will be ready with a better answer in the morning. I will examine you before you look at the fish."

This was disconcerting; not only must I think of my fish all night, studying, without the object before me, what this unknown but most visible feature might be, but also, without reviewing my new discoveries, I must give an exact account of them the next day. I had a bad memory; so I walked home by Charles River in a distracted state, with my two perplexities.

The cordial greeting from the professor the next morning was reassuring; here was a man who seemed to be quite as anxious as I that I should see for myself what he saw.

"Do you perhaps mean," I asked, "that the fish has symmetrical sides with paired organs?"

His thoroughly pleased, "Of course, of course!" repaid the wakeful hours of the previous night. After he had discoursed most happily and enthusiastically -- as he always did -- upon the importance of this point, I ventured to ask what I should do next.

"Oh, look at your fish!" he said, and left me again to my own devices. In a little more than an hour he returned and heard my new catalogue.

"That is good, that is good!" he repeated, "but that is not all; go on." And so for three long days, he placed that fish before my eyes, forbidding me to look at anything else, or to use any artificial aid. "Look, look, look," was his repeated injunction.

This was the best entomological lesson I ever had -- a lesson whose influence was extended to the details of every subsequent study; a legacy the professor has left to me, as he left it to many others, of inestimable value, which we could not buy, with which we cannot part.

A year afterwards, some of us were amusing ourselves with chalking outlandish beasts upon the blackboard. We drew prancing star-fishes; frogs in mortal combat; hydro-headed worms; stately craw-fishes, standing on their tails, bearing aloft umbrellas; and grotesque fishes, with gaping mouths and staring eyes. The professor came in shortly after, and was as much amused as any at our experiments. He looked at the fishes.

"*Haemulons*, every one of them," he said; "Mr. _____ drew them."

True; and to this day, if I attempt a fish, I can draw nothing but *Haemulons*.

The fourth day a second fish of the same group was placed beside the first, and I was bidden to point out the resemblances and differences between the two; another and another followed, until the entire family lay before me, and a whole legion of jars covered the table and surrounding shelves; the odor had become a pleasant perfume; and even now, the sight of an old six-inch worm-eaten cork brings fragrant memories!

The whole group of *Haemulon*s was thus brought into review; and whether engaged upon the dissection of the internal organs, preparation and examination of the bony framework, or the description of the various parts, Agassiz's training in the method of observing facts in their orderly arrangement, was ever accompanied by the urgent exhortation not to be content with them.

"Facts are stupid things," he would say, "until brought into connection with some general law."

At the end of eight months, it was almost with reluctance that I left these friends and turned to insects; but what I gained by this outside experience has been of greater value than years of later investigation in my favorite groups.

LEARNING TO OBSERVE

We can readily see that observation is a skill to be learned. How do we go about this learning? Where shall we start and how shall we proceed? Perhaps there is no simple answer, but practice is a necessity. The student who dedicated him/herself to the task of developing observational skills will grow and learn exponentially.

Good observers are those who ask themselves good questions. They intuitively know what they are looking for because they are asking the right questions.

There are six fundamental questions that we need to ask of the text under consideration. They are questions that must be a part of the observation stage, in the interpretation stage, in the correlation stage, and the application stage of Bible study. They are questions that should be woven into the very fabric of the student's life. They are: Who? What? When? Where? Why? And How?

Some of these questions have more than one part. "Who?" can mean who is writing, or who is being written to, or who is being written about, or who is doing the action. "Why?" could mean why is this person doing this, why is this included in the Bible, or why is this important?

As you practice observing, ask yourself the six questions and apply them to the Biblical text. If you need help you may wish to write these questions on a 3x5 card and look at them frequently as you read. Asking these questions will launch you down the road to making good observations.

We come now to direct observation of the Biblical text of Philemon. On the worksheets provided record as many observations as you can. Space has been provided between the lines. Before you start recording your observations, look at the key below. The suggested symbols may be used as a sort of observational shorthand."

Suggested Topics

General		Doctrinal	
Author	✍	Bible	📖
Recipients	✉	Dispensations / Ages	🕐
Re-occurring words	" "	God the Father	
Geography	🌐	Jesus Christ	✝
History	📜	Holy Spirit	🕊
Culture	🚩	Spirit Beings	👻
Subject	↘	Man	🧍
Action	⚡	Unrighteousness	♥
		Salvation	♡

Relational		Church	
Conflicts		Last Things	
One-anothers		Christian Life	
Attitudes			
Description		**Conditions**	
Figures of Speech		For, Therefore, Wherefore	
Love		Speculation	
Faith		Condition	

Observation Worksheet

1 Paul, a prisoner of Christ Jesus, and Timothy our brother, To Philemon our beloved friend and fellow laborer, 2 to the beloved Apphia, Archippus our fellow soldier, and to the church in your house:

3 Grace to you and peace from God our Father and the Lord Jesus Christ. 4 I thank my God, making mention of you always in my prayers, 5 hearing of your love and faith which you have toward the Lord Jesus and toward all the saints, 6 that the sharing of

your faith may become effective by the acknowledgment of every good thing which is in you in Christ Jesus. 7 For we have great joy and consolation in your love, because the hearts of the saints have been refreshed by you, brother. 8 Therefore, though I might be very bold in Christ to command you what is fitting, 9 yet for love's sake I rather appeal to you--being such a one as Paul, the aged, and now also a prisoner of Jesus Christ-- 10 I appeal to you for my son Onesimus, whom I have begotten while in my chains, 11 who once was unprofitable to you, but now is profitable to you and to me. 12 I am sending him back. You therefore receive him, that is, my own heart, 13 whom I wished to keep with me, that on your behalf he might minister to me in my chains for the gospel. 14 But without your consent I wanted to do nothing, that your good deed might not be by compulsion, as it were, but voluntary. 15 For perhaps he departed for a while for this purpose, that you might receive him forever, 16 no longer as a slave but more than a slave--a beloved brother, especially to me but how much more to you, both in the flesh and in the Lord. 17 If then you count me as a partner, receive him as you would me. 18 But if he has wronged you or owes anything, put that on my account. 19 I, Paul, am writing with my own hand. I will repay--not to mention to you that you owe me even your own self besides. 20 Yes, brother, let me have joy from you in the Lord; refresh my heart in the Lord. 21 Having confidence in your obedience, I write to you, knowing that you will do even more than I say. 22 But, meanwhile, also prepare a guest room for me, for I trust that through your prayers I shall be granted to you. 23 Epaphras, my fellow prisoner in Christ Jesus, greets you, 24 as do Mark, Aristarchus, Demas, Luke, my fellow laborers. 25 The grace of our Lord Jesus Christ be with your spirit. Amen.

Chapter Three
SKILL OF INTERPRETATION

The next step in the process of inductive Bible study is properly interpreting the Word of God. While observation answers the question, ―What does it say?" interpretation answers the question, ―What does it mean?" We will begin with a review of the fundamentals principles of interpretation and will then move on to the methods and tools that will help us to correctly interpret Scripture.

The study of Scripture will either stand or fall based on the interpretive method. I have often told my theology students that, "your method of hermeneutics will determine your theology." In other words, what you believe is based on how you interpret the Bible. Hermeneutics or your method of interpreting Scripture is the foundation on which all of one's beliefs rest.

There are primarily two methods of interpretation in Christendom. It is interesting to note that there are two primary theological systems in which most believers find themselves (whether they know it or not), and these two systems are each based on one of the two interpretive methods.

Allegorical Interpretation

An allegory may be defined as any statement that has a possible literal interpretation, but also has a deeper spiritual meaning. An allegory allows for a moral or spiritual interpretation. Allegorical interpretation is a system of interpretation in which possible literal interpretation is subjugated, set aside, viewed only as a vehicle for carrying what is perceived to be the more important moral or spiritual interpretation. In allegorical interpretation the historical aspect of the text is overcome or even ignored in favor of the moralistic lesson.

Unfortunately, this method allows all kinds of fantasy and speculation. More importantly, it denies that God, the giver of the revelation of Scripture, has a specific truth that He desires to convey, and further denies that He uses normal language to express it to

normal people. This method is leads to numerous problems:
1. According to the adherents of the Allegorical method, the average Christian is not "qualified" to interpret Scripture for themselves.
2. The reader becomes the *determiner of truth*, rather than the *recipient of truth*.
3. It denies the very concept of "Divine Revelation" as "the supernatural impartation of truth, from God to man, of that which man could not otherwise know."

Normal Interpretation

Normal interpretation is also known as literal, historical, grammatical interpretation.

By **literal**, we mean that the words and phrases are to be taken in their plain, normal, usual sense as they would be understood in any extra-biblical writing. This does not disallow the use of figurative language, but requires that figurative language be self evident, and interpreted in the normal sense. For example, "It is raining cats and dogs out there." No one, familiar with the normal use of the English language, would think that the speaker is declaring that animals are falling from the sky. No, they would understand that this figure of speech simply means that it is raining hard.

Historical interpretation means that we recognize that the human authors lived in a real time and a real place, and that the human recipients did so as well. Therefore, the intent of the authors (both human and Divine) is best understood by answering the question:

"What would the original recipients have understood this to mean?"

By **grammatical** interpretation we mean that the functions and rules of grammar are observed. Language is based upon grammatical principles that must be understood and followed; otherwise, there is no reliable means to communicate. This requires the reader to understand that there are grammatical devises such as, symbols, types, and parables. It then becomes the responsibility of the interpreter to properly deal with these devises in their context.

Consistent normal interpretation applies these principles of interpretation to every kind of Biblical literature, whether historical, poetic, or prophetic. There is no Biblical, linguistic, or grammatical reason to interpret prophecy differently that history. It was all written for the purpose to convey a message.

The Interpretive Approach of This Study

It is the doctrinal conviction of this author that the literal, historical, grammatical approach to the interpretation of Scripture is correct. This forms the content and conduct of this book, in which we will discover how this "normal" interpretive method should be applied to the study of Scripture.

The table which follows lists some of the principles of interpretation which the student should use in the interpretation of Scripture. They are catalogued according to general principles which correspond to the literal, historical, grammatical interpretation.

Principles of Interpretation
General Principles
1. God wrote the Bible because He intends on communicating to us. He intends that believers understand His Word (1 Cor 2:9-10).

2. God is all-knowing, all-wise, and all-powerful. Therefore, He is able to accomplish His intensions. The Bible is therefore profitable to men (2 Tim 3:16).

3. God is true and cannot contradict Himself (1 John 5:20; John 14:6; John 16:13, Heb 6:18).

4. Each believer bears the responsibility to be diligent in interpreting the Bible. He must cut a straight line through the Word of truth (2 Tim 2:15).

5. God intends that believers would both hear and do the Word of God. The primary purpose of Scripture is to change the heart, not to increase our knowledge (James 1:22).

6. The Bible is sufficient to equip believers for every good work that God requires them to do (2 Tim 3:17).

7. Believers need the assistance of the Holy Spirit to comprehend the Bible (John 16:13).

8. No other writing carries with it the quality of inspiration and authority as does the Bible. Therefore, Scripture is the best interpreter of Scripture (2 Tim 3:16).

9. The meaning of Scripture far outweighs personal experience (2 Peter 1:16-21).

Literal Principles

10. The actual words of Scripture are inspired in the original manuscripts, not just the ideas or concepts. Therefore, the believer must study each word as it is found in the original language (2 Tim 3:16; 1 Cor 2:12-13).

11. Words borrow their meaning from context. A word may have many meanings as it is used throughout a language (called semantic domain of a word) but it has only one meaning in any given context.

12. Literal speech includes figures of speech. A figure of speech is a deliberate distortion of reality to register a specific literary effect. A figure of speech must be obvious to the recipient in order for it to convey the intended meaning. In as much as God intends to communicate with believers, Biblical figures of speech are obvious to the informed student. The *informed* student of Scripture will make him/herself familiar with the common figures of speech used in language, so that they are recognized in Scripture and correctly interpreted.

Historical Principles

13. All Scripture was written to one or more specific (real) people. We must interpret the Scriptures as

they would be understood by those historical recipients.

14. God has dealt with different groups of people in different ways in different times. We cannot make the assumption that every historical group is treated identically (Gen 1:29; 2:16-17; cp. Gen 9:1-4; cp. Lev 11; cp. 1 Tim 4:1-5).

Grammatical Principles

15. The Scriptures gain their meaning through grammatical and syntactical relationships just as everyday speech or writing does. The interpreter must observe the use of singular, plural, tense, case, and other grammatical features of Scripture.

16. The most accurate way to interpret Scripture is to consider the grammar and syntax of the original languages of Biblical writings. The grammar and syntax of the target language may or may not accurately reflect the grammar of the original (especially if formal equivalence was not applied in the translation).

Principles of Interpreting Prophecy

17. Use all of the standard principles of interpretation.

18. Determine if a prophecy is fulfilled or unfulfilled:

    a. If the New Testament says that it is fulfilled, then it is! (e.g. Isa 7:17)

    b. The New Testament quotation of an Old Testament prophecy does not necessarily mean that it has been fulfilled.

19. Determine if the subject is treated elsewhere in Scripture. One passage does not necessarily tell it all (e.g. "The Day of the Lord").

20. Determine if the prophecy has more than one aspect of fulfillment. One may be local and soon after the prophecy is given. Another may be centuries and thousands of miles away. The theological name for multiple aspects in prophecy is "dual-fulfillment" (e.g. Isa 7:14; Joel 2:28).

21. Determine if the prophecy is conditional or unconditional.

22. Determine if there is an interpretation elsewhere in Scripture.

Principles for Interpreting Parables

23. The word parable comes from a compound Greek word [*para-ballo*] which means to throw alongside of.

24. Parables are used to hide truth from unbelievers while revealing truth to believers (Mat 13:10-13).

25. Parables have a reasonable earthly event placed alongside of a single spiritual or moral element.

26. The point of the parable is to teach a spiritual or moral truth.

27. There is only one spiritual or moral truth taught in a parable.

28. To interpret a parable, analyze the reasonable earthly event in terms of its own culture.

29. Look at the extended context to see if the parable is partially or completely interpreted in the context.

30. Determine the one main truth the parable is communicating.

31. Do not attempt to derive a spiritual truth from every element of the parable, just find the main truth.

32. Look carefully at the recipients of the parable to determine its applicability.

Principles for Interpreting Types

33. A type is an illustration based on the Old Testament character, event, or institution, which, while having a reality and purpose in Biblical history, is a Devine foreshadowing of things to come.

34. There are five essential elements in a type:

    a. It is an illustration

    b. It is based in the Old Testament

    c. It has reality and purpose in Biblical history

    d. It is of Divine design

    e. It is a foreshadowing of future things

35. To be a type it must be evident from Scripture itself

   a. The Scripture says so (e.g. Adam is a type of Christ. Rom 5:14).

   b. It may be based in the interchange of names (The Passover was a type of Christ. 1 Cor 5:7).

36. Interpret types historically before you interpret them typically.

37. The type presents a general resemblance to its antitype.

38. Nothing of an evil nature can be a type of that which is good.

The Interpretation of Symbols

39. A symbol is a timeless figure of speech in which one item is used to represent another.

40. In order to be a symbol the actual statement must be impossible or contradicted by Scripture. (e.g. Satan is called a dragon in Rev 20:2. Scripture identifies Satan as a spirit being, not a physical dragon, therefore, "dragon" is a symbol).

PERSPECTIVE

Interpretation may be carried out from different perspectives. One common perspective in Bible study is the perspective which approaches an entire unit at one time. This may be a section of Scripture such as the Pentateuch or an entire book of the Bible. This perspective is called *synthesis*.

Another perspective in Biblical study approaches the Word of God line by line and word by word. This detailed perspective is called *analysis*. Both synthesis and analysis are legitimate and valuables ways to approach the study of God's Word. Synthesis focuses on the "forest" as a whole while analysis emphasizes the individual "trees." You will discover as we proceed that some methods of Bible study are "big picture" studies and others are "detail" studies. A thorough study of the Bible will include both synthesis and analysis.

In this course we will organize our study around the three aspects of normal interpretation; we will learn methods that help us to be literal, others that focus on historical study, and others that ensure grammatical interpretation. Both synthetic and analytical methods will be employed as appropriate.

LITERAL INTERPRETATION

Which methods of Bible study focus on literal interpretation? Well, all of them should! But some methods simply acknowledge that the Scripture means just what it says. We will begin with synthesis, the big picture, as it applies to the book of Philemon. We will learn how to title paragraphs, discover the theme of the book, re-title the paragraphs in light of the theme and chart the results in a synthetic chart.

Paragraph Titling

A paragraph is a group of related sentences, organized around some central theme or idea. Most paragraphs have a topic sentence which identifies the theme or central idea of the paragraph.

Many grammarians consider the paragraph to be the fundamental unit of expression. The value of creating a title for each paragraph is that we then discover the meaning of each fundamental building blocks of a book of the Bible. This represents literal interpretation because it is based on what the text actually says. A series of paragraph titles will assist us in discovering the theme of the book.

The Bible was not written with paragraph breaks in it. Therefore you must either make your own paragraph breaks or accept the paragraphs suggested by the editors of you particular translation. Different Bible translations and different study Bibles suggest different paragraph divisions. It is helpful to read the introductory material in your Bible to discover how the editors determined the locations of paragraph breaks.

Similarly, we must remember that the chapter and verse divisions were added for convenience in locating Scriptures and are not inspired. Consequently, you may ignore them when making paragraph divisions.

Paragraph titling is much like writing headlines for a newspaper. The newspaper headlines attempt to capture the essence of the article in just a few words for the reader. The paragraph title does much the same thing.

A good paragraph title does not attempt to include all of the details of the paragraph, but must be broad enough to encompass all that the paragraph addresses, it should summarize the paragraph.

Paragraph Titling Worksheets

Consider that you have the following elements in a paragraph:

Cat Blue; Dog Pink; Monkey Green; Pig Orange

Several possible paragraph titles commend themselves:
- Colors
- Animals
- Colored animals
- Animals of Color

Suppose that you had the following paragraph elements:

JOY   PEACE   LOVE
What might be a good paragraph title for the above?

You might have written:
    Fruit of the Spirit
    Godly Qualities
    Christian Character Traits

Now, let's add two more elements:
JOY PEACE LOVE FAITH HOPE
What would you title this?

This should have changed your title. Fruit of the Spirit would no longer work because "hope" is not listed as part of the fruit of the Spirit in Paul's letter to the Galatians. So we must expand the title to encompass a broader subject.

Let's try another one. Suppose the elements of a paragraph are:

BASKETBALL   FOOTBALL   BASEBALL
Some possible paragraph titles would be:

Did you consider different perspectives? Some possible titles might be:
- Team Sports
- Kinds of Balls
- Sporting Events

Here is an exercise to help you view a paragraph from different perspectives. Consider Philemon 1:1-3. Read this paragraph several times. Then complete the following:

1. Write a possible paragraph title.

2. Put yourself in the shoes of the human author. Write a paragraph title from his perspective.

3. Now write a title from the perspective of the recipient (Philemon) of the letter.

4. Write a title from your own personal perspective as a modern day reader.

5. Which is the better perspective? Why?

When we interpret scripture we always seek to discover the intent of the human author in writing the Scripture. In the case of the letter to Philemon, we ask, "what did Paul mean to say?'

Though we cannot read the mind of the human author of Scripture, we must do some work in order to ascertain his true intention. However, it is important to remember that the human author is only on half of the writing team. Because of the supernatural supervision of the Divine Author (2 Peter 1:21) we know that the Bible says what God intended for it to say.

Because God is the perfect communicator, and because we cannot read the mind of the human author, we are forced to ask another question. "What would the original recipients of this letter have understood it to say?" Since God is the Perfect Communicator, and since He supervised the communication process, the original recipients would have understood what God intended.

Based on this reasoning, the best perspective to use in titling a paragraph is to ask "How would the original recipients of this Scripture have understood this passage?"

In just a moment we will begin titling the paragraphs of Philemon, But first let us consider two more guidelines concerning paragraph titling. When we title a paragraph, the title should be unique to that paragraph. One could title every paragraph "Instructions from Paul." But that would not accomplish our goal of better understanding the passage. It may be tempting to take the easy route, but it will not be profitable. ***Do the work!***

Another guideline that will help in the overall process is to keep your titles short. Generally speaking most paragraph titles should be no longer than five words. Though this rule may seem arbitrary, it has an important purpose. The goal is to have a paragraph title that summarizes the information in the paragraph.

When you title a paragraph you do not need to write in complete sentences. Look at your local newspaper to get an idea of how headlines are written. We should word paragraph titles in a similar way.

Now we are ready to title the paragraphs of Philemon. Some paragraph divisions have been supplied for you. Remember, these divisions are not inspired and you may change them if you choose.

PARAGRAPH TITLING EXERCISE

Using the paragraph divisions below (or create your own), title each paragraph in five words or less.

1:1-3

1:4:7

1:8-16

1:17-22

1:23-25

DISCOVERING THE THEME OF THE BOOK

Most books have a central theme or idea that the author is developing. The theme is the central, overall message of the book. When we do Bible synthesis, a look at the big picture, we try to discover the theme of the book. Once the theme has been discovered, we will then interpret each passage in light of that overall theme.

Look back at your paragraph titles. Each title should accurately reflect what that paragraph is about. If you were to add the paragraph titles together, you should discover the theme of the book as a whole.

In the longer books of the Bible there may be several "sub-themes." These divisions are like major sections in a manual, each one covering a major area. But just like paragraph titles, you can add up these "sub-themes" and ascertain the overall subject of the book.

Use the following page to record some possible themes for the book of Philemon. Then select the theme that you feel best describes the overall purpose of the book. Like a paragraph title, a theme should be stated in five or less words, and should be large enough to encompass the entire book, but specific enough so that it summarizes that particular Bible book.

THEME EXERCISE

Write several possible themes for Philemon in the space below. Remember to use the different perspectives (author, recipient, etc…).

Possible themes for Philemon:

Now select the one that best expresses the purpose of the book.

Why did you select this one?

Paragraph Re-Titling

So far we have titled each of the paragraphs of the book of Philemon and we have discovered the overall theme. Now it is time to see how our individual paragraph titles manifest the overall theme. I know that this may seem redundant, but keep in mind, you cannot handle the text of Scripture too much. The more you apply these tools to a passage, the better you will understand it.

In this part of the process we re-read and if necessary, re-title each of the paragraphs with the overall theme in view. We ask the question, "How does this paragraph reflect or contribute to the theme?"

Some books of the Bible are written very "tightly." That is, each paragraph in each chapter seems to hammer home the central idea of the book. Other books of Scripture seem to be more of a collection of mini-themes brought together. If we were titling the chapters of the book of Proverbs we would discover that the authors treat a variety of subjects including, wisdom, sexual purity, family relationships, work ethic, money management, child-training, and much more. We might decide that the overall theme of the book is, "Practical Wisdom for Daily Living," or "Godly Principles for Wise Living." Either of these titles would be broad enough to encompass all that is broached in the book of Proverbs.

Because Proverbs has more than one human author, and due to the nature of the book itself, it is structurally loose. We therefore select a thematic statement that covers all of it. It would be difficult (but not impossible) to title each paragraph reflecting the overall theme.

NOTE: Bible study is not necessarily easy. There will be times that you seem stuck, or you may believe that all of your hard work is for nothing. Take heart, and remember, the more that you handle the text, the more the Holy Spirit will illuminate.

Much of the value in this kind of study lies not in the specific thematic statement that you record but in the process of wrestling with the text until you gain understanding of what the author is saying to the original recipients. In this course of study the value lies more in the process than in the product.

PARAGRAPH RE-TITLING EXERCISE

It may be necessary to review and re-title your paragraphs, now that you have discovered the theme. Write your theme for the book of Philemon below. Then review and if necessary re-title each paragraph in light of the theme.

Theme:

1:1-3

1:4-7

1:8-16

1:17-22

1: 23-25

EVALUATION

How did you re-titles turn out? Did you find yourself changing some or all of them in light of the theme? Do they accurately reflect the theme? Many times there will be a common thread in the re-titles. This may be the name of a person like Paul or Philemon. Or it may be a word that describes a characteristic, a relationship or ministry, such as grace, peace, love, preach, teach…

In some cases I go through the titling—theme—re-titling process two or three times, maybe even more before I am pleased with the results. Remember that the Bible is a complex book that we can and should study for our entire lives without exhausting its riches.

Sometimes I come back to a book of the Bible years later and develop a new and more comprehensive understanding of its theme. When this happens, it excites me, because it is evidence that I have gained in my spiritual maturity since the last time I visited that book.

At this time in our study allow me to take a moment and share with you some encouragement. I understand that it can seem a daunting task to tackle a Book of Scripture and conduct an inductive study. Already you may be feeling overwhelmed and even a bit frustrated. My advice to you is to take a deep breath, relax and enjoy the process of discovery. And, keep in mind that you will not understand every aspect of every word of a passage of Scripture the first time that you study it. Personal Bible study is about discovery, re-discovery and delving deeper and deeper, all the while understand that you may never reach the bottom. What I am trying to say is that it is more about the journey than it is the destination.

CHARTING A BIBLE BOOK

When you are satisfied that you have a pretty good picture of what the Book that you are studying is all about you will want to record that in chart form. A synthetic chart is a snapshot that records the paragraph titles and overall theme in a single simple diagram.

There are many different types of charts but they basically all boil down to two kinds, synthetic (over view) and analytical (detail view).

Following I have supplied a sample synthetic chart for the book of Titus.

1:1-4	1:5-9	1:10-16	2:1-10	2:11-14	2:15-3:2	3:3-7	3:8-11	3:12-15
Salutation	The Elders	The False Teachers	Conduct of Saints	Conduct in Grace	Conduct in Civil Law	Conduct in Salvation	Conduct in Respect to Error	finale
Commendation	Constituents		Conduct					Conclusion
CONDUCT OF THE CHURCH AT CRETE								

Using your theme and paragraph titles, create a synthetic chart of the Book of Philemon below.

SYNTACTICAL ANALYSIS

We now zoom in with our camera, from looking at the forest to looking at individual trees. We are moving from synthesis to analysis. In this particular study we will perform syntactical analysis, which may sound complicated but is actually very helpful and motivating in Biblical study.

What is Syntax?

Syntax is the ~~orderly~~ arrangement of words and their relation to one another to convey meaning in a sentence.[3]" When one is plunged into a foreign culture, he or she will inevitably pick up on the meaning of many of that culture's words. One could overhear a conversation about a chair, and know that the speakers are discussing the chair. However, without *syntax*, the eavesdropper may not know if they were talking about buying a chair, selling a chair, fixing a chair or asking someone else to sit in a chair.

Greek Versus English Syntax

English is called a linear language. That is, in the English language, the function of a word in a sentence is conveyed by its position in a sentence. Notice the following sentences.

1. The dog bit the boy.
2. The boy bit the dog.

---

[3] Ray Summers, *Essentials of New Testament Greek, Revised*, Nashville: Broadman & Holman, 1995. P29

In the above example each sentences has exactly the same number of words. And the words have the same meaning. However, the order of the words determine the overall meaning expressed.

In the Koine Greek language (an inflected language), the language of the New Testament, syntax related to nouns is conveyed primarily by inflection, or form. Each noun has a suffix (called it ending), to point to its intended use in the sentence. This syntactical function is assisted by other words including conjunctions and prepositions.

Greek is more specific. In Greek the function of a noun in a sentence is determined by its ending. A noun functioning as the subject will have a *nominative* ending, where a noun functioning as an object will have an *accusative* ending.

To understand the syntax of the Greek New Testament, the student must either study two to three years of Koine Greek or be aware of the existence of and proper use of the vast Greek tools available. One such tool is a good Greek grammar such as *Essentials of New Testament Greek* by Ray Summers. It is also helpful to use a good analytical Greek lexicon. An analytical Greek lexicon tells the English reader which case ending is used on every noun. Using these two tools together the student can apply simple rules of grammar and syntax.

It is beyond the scope of this book to teach the intricacies of Greek syntax, but we can use an interlinear Greek-English New Testament to identify some of the key connecting words used in the Greek text.

INTRODUCING KEY CONNECTING WORDS

In this study we will learn about some key connecting words from the Greek New Testament. Though this may seem very alien and a bit scary to you, this study will greatly multiply the your understanding of the Bible.

After we have explained each of the connecting words following, giving you biblical examples of their use, we will produce a chart of the words so that you can see them all together. Then you will apply what you have learned by discovering these Greek connecting words as they appear in Philemon.

KEY CONNECTING WORDS

καί   1. Greek: καί   English: kai
Pronounced: kai
This is the most common Greek connecting word. It is often translated "and" but it has different meanings in different contexts. There are three major uses of καί:
  a. Adjunctive or additive. In this use καί adds two different things together. When we say the flag is "red and white and blue" the word "and" is adding together different elements. In this use καί adds together different elements that have the same grammatical weight and form: two nouns, two verbs,

two phrases, two clauses, etc. (2 Corinthians 1:1; Ephesians 1:2; Philippians 1:21.

b. Ascensive, intensive, or emphatic. In this use the word καὶ is used between two nouns or pronouns that refer to the same thing. The first noun introduces the subject; the second one intensifies the use by providing more information about the first. Galatians 1:4 is an example of this use:

> ...who gave Himself for our sins, that he might deliver us from this present evil age, according to the will of our God *and* Father.

In this verse "God" and "Father" refer to the same person. Therefore, this is an Ascensive use of καὶ. The Ascensive use can, in some circumstances, be translated "even."

c. Continuative, or transitional. This use of the word represents poor English grammar but it works perfectly in Greek. In this use the word καὶ continues the narrative without suggesting any particular relationship between what went before and what follows after. When you find an English sentence that begins with "and" where the Greek word is και, you probably have this use of και. In this use it is sometimes translated "then." 1 Corinthians 3:1; Revelation 7:2.

δε Greek: δε   English: de
Pronounced: dė
This word may be translated "and," "but" or "now." However, it always has a continuative or transitional meaning, just as the continuative use of και does.[4] This word will always stand second or third in the Greek sentence rather than first. Galatians 2:22; Galatians 2:6; Galatians 2:11. The word δε is used 2870 times in the New Testament.

αλλα Greek: αλλα   English: alla
Pronounced: allah
Contrastive, or adversative. This is the word in Greek which places two terms against one another. It is usually

---

[4] Though not thoroughly reflected in the English, και carries a more emphatic use than the other connective conjunctives.

translated ‑but." In English we would say, ‑not up but down," or ‑not the boy but the girl." Galatians 1:17; 1 Peter 1:15. Used 637 times in the New Testament.

η   Greek: η   English: a
Pronounced: ā – as in d<u>ay</u>
Choice. This word, translated ‑or" in English gives a choice. If I say, ‑you may have the red one or the blue one" it presents the recipient with a choice between two. Matthew 10:37; Luke 2:24. Used 357 times in the New Testament.

γαρ   Greek: γαρ   English: gar
Pronounced: gar
Explanatory, or continuation. This word is explanatory when occurring at the beginning of a clause. This word, may be translate ‑for," ‑therefore," or ‑wherefore." It shows that what follows explains that which proceeds. This is one of the more useful of the Greek connecting words because it alerts the savvy reader to an important point of syntax. This is the reason for the rule, ‑when you see a _for,' _therefore,' or a _wherefore,' you have to find out what it's there for." Paul is especially fond of this word, and it helps the Bible student to make sense of his long sentences. This

word, like δε, always stands second or third in the Greek sentence. Used 1067 times in the New Testament.

κατα Greek: κατα   English: kata
Pronounced: kata
Subordinated to. This Greek word is nearly always translated "according to" and indicates that the thing discussed is logically subordinated to that which follows. It is important to note that κατα is never used to show physical relationship, but logical relationship. Ephesians 1:5,7. Used 480 times in the New Testament.

δια Greek: δια   English: dia
Pronounced: dia
Logical Conclusion, inferential. This word is generally translated by either "wherefore" or "therefore" and gives the logical conclusion result of a discussion. Eg. "It is raining, therefore (δια) you will get wet." It often appears as the first word in a sentence and may appear with a capitol letter (Δια). James 1:21; 1 Peter 2:14. Used 646 times in the New Testament.

ουν

Greek: ουν English: oun
Pronounced: oon
Logical Conclusion, inferential. May also act as a continuative or transitional. As a logical conclusion ουν is considered to be weaker than δια, James 5:7. As a continuative it is often translated "then" as in Matthew 7:11 or Mark 11:31. In this use it may also be translated "now," John 19:29, Acts 1:18. This word, like δε and γαρ, never stands first in a sentence. Remember, when it is translated "then" or "now" it is not referring to time but is giving a logical conclusion to a proposition. Used 489 times in the New Testament.

ινα

Greek: ινα English: hina
Pronounced: heena
Purpose. This word is nearly always translated "that" or "in order that." It shows the purpose for which something is done and is therefore important in decoding Greek syntax. 1 Thessalonians 5:10; 1 John 2:1. Used 350 times in the New Testament.

ει

Greek: ει English: ei
Pronounced: Ī
First Class Condition. This word is used with a verb in the "indicative" to show a

first class condition. A first class condition in Greek is a condition that is assumed to be true. It can be translated "since." Suppose someone told you that they were going to the store. You might say, "If you are going to the store, would you please get me a newspaper?" In this type of statement you use the word "if" even though you assume it is true. "Since you are going to the store..." 1 Corinthians 15:2; Galatians 5:25. Used 291 times in the New Testament.

ει...αν Greek: ει...αν English: ean
Pronounced: e-an the "e" as in m**e**t
Second Class Condition. These words are used together with a verb in the "subjunctive" mood to show a condition that is not true, or contrary to fact. The ellipsis (dots) mean that other words will occur in the sentence between the ει and the αν. We say this in English using the tone of our voice or in written English, by the use of the subjunctive verb. Suppose I write, "If I were a five foot tall Japanese woman..." I am not. I am a white male who stands just over six foot. The use of "were" is a flag for you that this is a condition contrary to fact. I am indicating that I am NOT a five foot Japanese woman. John 5:46;

1 Corinthians 2:8. Used 191 times in the New Testament.

εαν   Greek: εαν   English: ean
Pronounced: e-an the "e" as in m<u>e</u>t
Third Class Condition. This word is used with a verb in the "subjunctive" to show uncertainty. This is the true "if." For instance, "If it rains today..." This condition admits a lack of knowledge on the part of the speaker. All three conditions are generally translated "if" in the English, so the use of an interlinear is highly recommended, to see if the word is ει (first class), ει...αν (second class), or εαν (third class). Examples of the third class condition are found in Matthew 4:9, 1 John 1:9. It is used 275 times in the New Testament.

These are not all of the connecting words found in the Greek New Testament. A mastery of these words, however, will give the English Bible student a big head start on Greek syntax and will help him or her to understand the structure of "discussion" in the New Testament. The Bible student will find the following chart a great help as you can see these connecting words in a single glance.

GREEK KEY CONNECTING WORDS CHART

Greek Connecting Word	English Translation	Basic Meaning
και	And	Adjunctive, additive,
και	And	Ascentive, intensive, emphatic
και	and, then	Continuative, transitional
δε	and, now, but	Continuative, transitional
αλλα	But	Contrastive, adversative
η	Or	Choice
γαρ	For	Explanatory
κατα	according to	Subordinated to, logical relationship
δια	therefore, wherefore	Logical conclusion, inferential
ουν	therefore	Logical conclusion, inferential
ουν	then, now	Continuative, transitional
ινα	that, in order that	Purpose
ει	if, since	First Class Condition Assumed to be true
ει...αν	if	Second Class Condition Contrary to fact, false
εαν	if	Third Class Condition Uncertain. The true "if"

SYNTACTICAL ANALYSIS EXERCISE

You are now prepared to use what you have learned to do a syntactical analysis of Philemon. In this study you will use a Greek-English Interlinear New Testament to discover the connecting words in the book of Philemon. You will want to refer to the "Greek Key Connecting Words Chart" on the previous page.

Place this chart next to your interlinear and carefully read through the book of Philemon. Every time you come to a possible key connecting word in English, look up the word in the interlinear portion to see if it is one that we have studied. If it is, list it on the next page, recording the verse number, the English word, the Greek word, and the basic meaning in their respective columns.

SYNTACTICAL ANALYSIS OF PHILEMON

Verse	English Word	Greek Word	Basic Meaning

The Epistle of Paul the Apostle to
PHILEMON

ΠΡΟΣ ΦΙΛΗΜΟΝΑ
TO PHILEMON

Paul Greets Philemon

1 Παῦλος, δέσμιος Χριστοῦ Ἰησοῦ, καὶ Τιμόθεος ὁ
Paul, a prisoner of Christ Jesus, and Timothy the
ἀδελφός,
brother,

Φιλήμονι τῷ ἀγαπητῷ καὶ συνεργῷ ἡμῶν 2 καὶ
To Philemon ²beloved ³and ⁴fellow ⁵worker ¹our and
Ἀπφίᾳ τῇ ἀγαπητῇ ᵃ καὶ Ἀρχίππῳ τῷ συστρατιώτῃ ἡμῶν
to Apphia the beloved and to Archippus ²fellow ³soldier ¹our
καὶ τῇ κατ' οἶκόν σου ἐκκλησίᾳ·
and to the ²at ⁴house ³your ¹church:

3 Χάρις ὑμῖν καὶ εἰρήνη ἀπὸ Θεοῦ Πατρὸς ἡμῶν καὶ
Grace to you and peace from God Father ¨ our and
Κυρίου Ἰησοῦ Χριστοῦ.
the Lord Jesus Christ.

1 Paul, a prisoner of Christ Jesus, and Timothy our brother,

To Philemon our beloved *friend* and fellow laborer, 2 to the beloved Apphia, Archippus our fellow soldier, and to the church in your house:

3 Grace to you and peace from God our Father and the Lord Jesus Christ.

Paul Commends Philemon's Love and Faith

4 Εὐχαριστῶ τῷ Θεῷ μου πάντοτε μνείαν σου
I thank - God ¨ my always ²mention ³of ⁴you
ποιούμενος ἐπὶ τῶν προσευχῶν μου, 5 ἀκούων σου τὴν
¹making in - prayers ¨ my, hearing of your -
ἀγάπην καὶ τὴν πίστιν ἣν ἔχεις πρὸς τὸν Κύριον Ἰησοῦν
love and - faith which you have toward the Lord Jesus
καὶ εἰς πάντας τοὺς ἁγίους, 6 ὅπως ἡ κοινωνία τῆς
and toward all the saints, that the sharing of
πίστεώς σου ἐνεργὴς γένηται ἐν ἐπιγνώσει παντὸς
of faith ¨ your ³effective ¹may ²become in full knowledge of every
ἀγαθοῦ τοῦ ἐν ἡμῖν ᵇ εἰς Χριστὸν Ἰησοῦν. 7 Χάριν
good thing the one in us for Christ Jesus. ⁵thanksgiving
which is
γὰρ ἔχομεν πολλὴν ᶜ καὶ παράκλησιν ἐπὶ τῇ ἀγάπῃ σου,
¹For ²we ³have ⁴much and encouragement over - love ¨ your,
ὅτι τὰ σπλάγχνα τῶν ἁγίων ἀναπέπαυται διὰ σοῦ,
because the inward parts of the saints have been refreshed through you,
affections
ἀδελφέ.
brother.

4 I thank my God, making mention of you always in my prayers,
5 hearing of your love and faith which you have toward the Lord Jesus and toward all the saints,
6 that the sharing of your faith may become effective by the acknowledgment of every good thing which is in you in Christ Jesus.
7 For we have great joy and consolation in your love, because the hearts of the saints have been refreshed by you, brother.

Paul Intercedes for Onesimus

8 Διό, πολλὴν ἐν Χριστῷ παρρησίαν ἔχων
Therefore, ²much ⁴in ⁵Christ ³boldness ¹having
ἐπιτάσσειν σοι τὸ ἀνῆκον, 9 διὰ τὴν ἀγάπην
to command you the fitting thing, on account of - love
what is fitting,
μᾶλλον παρακαλῶ, τοιοῦτος ὢν ὡς Παῦλος πρεσβύτης,
rather I appeal, ²such ³a ⁴one ¹being as Paul an old man,

8 Therefore, though I might be very bold in Christ to command you what is fitting,
9 yet for love's sake I rather appeal *to you* — being such a one as Paul, the aged, and now also

---

ᵃ(2) NU reads ἀδελφῇ, sister. ᵇ(6) TR reads ὑμῖν, you. ᶜ(7) NU reads χαρὰν γὰρ πολλὴν ἔσχον, For I had much joy.

a prisoner of Jesus Christ —
10 I appeal to you for my son
Onesimus, whom I have begotten *while* in my chains.
11 who once was unprofitable to you, but now is profitable to you and to me.
12 I am sending him back. You therefore receive him, that is, my own heart,
13 whom I wished to keep with me, that on your behalf he might minister to me in my chains for the gospel.
14 But without your consent I wanted to do nothing, that your good deed might not be by compulsion, as it were, but voluntary.
15 For perhaps he departed for a while for this *purpose*, that you might receive him forever,
16 no longer as a slave but more than a slave — a beloved brother, especially to me but how much more to you, both in the flesh and in the Lord.
17 If then you count me as a partner, receive him as *you would* me.
18 But if he has wronged you or owes anything, put that on my account.
19 I, Paul, am writing with my own hand. I will repay — not to mention to you that you owe me even your own self besides.
20 Yes, brother, let me have joy from you in the Lord; refresh my heart in the Lord.
21 Having confidence in your obedience, I write to you, knowing that you will do even more than I say.
22 But, meanwhile, also prepare a guest room for me, for I trust that through your prayers I shall be granted to you.

---

d(12) NU reads σοι, *to you*, for συ δε, thus adding to v. 12a: *whom I sent back to you*. e(12) NU omits προσλαβου, *receive* (see previous note). f(20) NU reads Χριστω, *Christ*.

νυνὶ δὲ καὶ δέσμιος Ἰησοῦ Χριστοῦ. 10 Παρακαλῶ σε
now " but also a prisoner of Jesus Christ.   I appeal to   you
περὶ   τοῦ ἐμοῦ τέκνου, ὃν   ἐγέννησα ἐν τοῖς δεσμοῖς μου,
concerning   my   child,   whom I begot   in   bonds "   my,
Ὀνήσιμον, 11 τὸν   ποτέ σοι   ἄχρηστον, νυνὶ δὲ σοὶ   καὶ
Onesimus,   the *one* once to you unprofitable, now " but to you and
                  who was
ἐμοὶ εὔχρηστον, 12 ὃν   ἀνέπεμψα. Σὺ δὲ^d αὐτόν, τοῦτ᾽ ἔστι
to me is useful,   whom I sent back. You then ²him, ³this ⁴is
                                                              that
τὰ ἐμὰ σπλάγχνα, προσλαβοῦ·^e 13 ὃν   ἐγὼ ἐβουλόμην
- ⁵my ⁶inward ⁷parts, ¹receive;   whom I   wished
  very heart,
πρὸς ἐμαυτὸν κατέχειν, ἵνα   ὑπὲρ   σοῦ διακονῇ
with myself   to retain, in order that on behalf of you he might serve
μοι ἐν τοῖς δεσμοῖς τοῦ εὐαγγελίου. 14 Χωρὶς δὲ τῆς σῆς
me in the bonds   of the gospel.   without " But -   your
γνώμης οὐδὲν ἠθέλησα ποιῆσαι, ἵνα   μὴ ὡς κατὰ
consent ²nothing ¹I ⁴wished ³to ⁴do, in order that ¹not ²as ⁷by
ἀνάγκην τὸ ἀγαθόν σου ᾖ   ἀλλὰ κατὰ ἑκούσιον.
⁸necessity - ²good ¹your ³might ⁵be but   by *being* voluntary.
15 Τάχα γὰρ διὰ   τοῦτο ἐχωρίσθη   πρὸς ὥραν
perhaps " For on account of this he was taken away for   an hour
                                                            a time
ἵνα   αἰώνιον αὐτὸν ἀπέχῃς,   16 οὐκέτι ὡς δοῦλον
in order that ³eternally ⁴him ¹you ²might ³keep,   no longer as a slave
ἀλλ᾽ ὑπὲρ δοῦλον, ἀδελφὸν ἀγαπητόν, μάλιστα ἐμοί,
but beyond a slave, a brother " beloved,   especially to me,
πόσῳ   δὲ μᾶλλον σοὶ καὶ ἐν σαρκὶ καὶ ἐν Κυρίῳ.
²how ³much ¹but ⁴more to you both in *the* flesh and in *the* Lord.

Paul Encourages Philemon's Obedience

17 Εἰ οὖν με ἔχεις   κοινωνόν, προσλαβοῦ αὐτὸν ὡς
   If then ³me ¹you ²have as a partner, receive   him   as
                                                         count
ἐμέ. 18 Εἰ δέ τι   ἠδίκησέ σε ἢ ὀφείλει,   τοῦτο
me.   if " But *in* anything he wronged you or owes *anything*, ²this
ἐμοὶ ἐλλόγει. 19 Ἐγὼ Παῦλος ἔγραψα τῇ ἐμῇ χειρί,
³to ⁴me ¹charge.   I   Paul   wrote -   with my *own* hand,
                                                   am writing
"Ἐγὼ ἀποτίσω" — ἵνα   μὴ λέγω σοι ὅτι καὶ σεαυτόν
"I   will repay" — in order that not " I say to you that even yourself
                          lest
μοι   προσοφείλεις! 20 Ναί, ἀδελφέ, ἐγώ σου
³to ⁴me ¹you ²owe!   Yes, brother, ²I ⁵from ⁶you
ὀναίμην   ἐν Κυρίῳ· ἀνάπαυσόν μου τὰ σπλάγχνα ἐν
¹may ³have ⁴profit in *the* Lord; refresh   my -   inward parts in
                                                                affections
Κυρίῳ.^f
the Lord.

21 Πεποιθὼς   τῇ ὑπακοῇ   σου ἔγραψά σοι,
   Having been persuaded of - obedience " your I wrote   to you,
   Being confident of   I am writing
εἰδὼς ὅτι καὶ ὑπὲρ ὃ   λέγω ποιήσεις. 22 Ἅμα   δὲ
knowing that even beyond what I say you will do.   meanwhile " But
καὶ ἑτοίμαζέ μοι ξενίαν,   ἐλπίζω γὰρ ὅτι διὰ   τῶν
also prepare me a guest room, ²I ¹hope ¹for that through -
προσευχῶν ὑμῶν χαρισθήσομαι   ὑμῖν.
prayers "   your I will be graciously given to you.

Paul's Farewell

23 Ἀσπάζονταί σε Ἐπαφρᾶς ὁ συναιχμάλωτός μου ἐν
There greet you Epaphras - ²fellow ³captive ¹my in
Χριστῷ Ἰησοῦ, **24** Μάρκος, Ἀρίσταρχος, Δημᾶς, Λουκᾶς, οἱ
Christ Jesus, Mark, Aristarchus, Demas, Luke, -
συνεργοί μου.
²fellow ³workers ¹my.
25 Ἡ χάρις τοῦ Κυρίου ἡμῶν Ἰησοῦ Χριστοῦ μετὰ τοῦ
The grace - of Lord - our Jesus Christ be with -
πνεύματος ὑμῶν. Ἀμήν.^κ
spirit ° your. Amen.
So be it.

PHILEMON 25

23 Epaphras, my fellow prisoner in Christ Jesus, greets you,
24 as do Mark, Aristarchus, Demas, Luke, my fellow laborers.
25 The grace of our Lord Jesus Christ be with your spirit. Amen.

κ(25) NU omits Αμην, Amen.

The Unashamed

The Rhetorical Method

Rhetoric is the classical art of influencing the thoughts of another. The rhetorical method of Bible study is that method in which the special literary uses of language, including genre and figures of speech are examined.

This is an important subject of study because it is impossible to rightly understand written communication without considering both genre and figures of speech. When we say that we practice "literal" interpretation, we are saying that we interpret in light of the common or "normal" use of language. This method of interpretation considers figures of speech just as they are used in the common speech of the author and recipients.

Rhetorical study is also important because the Bible was specifically written to influence our thoughts and to spur us to appropriate action (James 1:22). We must take pains to ascertain that which Scripture is enticing us to do.

Genre

Literary genre is "a class or category of artistic endeavor having a particular form, content, technique, or the like."[5] Dr. Roy Zuck, Author and Theologian, identifies seven literary genres in the Bible.[6] These are:

> ➢ Legal
> ➢ Narrative
> ➢ Poetry

---
[5] *Webster's American Dictionary*. New York: Random House, 1997. s.v. "genre."
[6] Roy Zuck, *Basic Bible Interpretation*. Wheaton: Victor Books, 1991. pp 126-142.

- Wisdom Literature
- Gospels
- Logical Discourse
- Prophetic Literature

Legal
The word legal refers to the law, the first five books of the Old Testament (the Pentateuch). But when used of literary genre it refers to any writing that gives laws. Zuck refers to apodictic law, the ―Thou shalt nots" of the Ten Commandments, and the casuistic law which addresses specific cases.

Narrative Genre
A narrative is a story. In the Bible stories are selected and included in order to teach believers truth. While each story has a real, historical value, they have been included in the Word of God to both inform man of God's standards and to conform him to them. Zuck describes the pattern of narratives:

> Narratives usually follow a pattern in which a problem occurs near the beginning of the narrative, with increasing complications that reach a climax. And then the narrative moves toward a solution to the problem and concludes with the problem solved.[7]

---
[7] Ibid, 128.

Zuck lists six types of narrative including, tragedy, epic, romance, heroic, satire, and polemic. These classifications generally answer the question, ―What is the point of this narrative?"

Biblical Poetry

When we think of Biblical poetry our attention is immediately directed to the five Old Testament books which are called the poetical books: Job, Psalms, Proverbs, Ecclesiastes, and the Song of Solomon. But there is much poetry in other books as well. Some translations of the Bible have typeset the poetry to make it distinctive to the reader.

Hebrew poetry is not like English poetry. English poetry is often marked by repeated sounds and meter. Hebrew poetry, on the other hand, is marked by thought parallelism. Some of the major kinds of parallelism are:

➢ Synonymous Parallelism. The second line restates the first line using different words but the same ideas. Psalm 3:1

➢ Synthetic Parallelism. The second line adds to or completes the thought introduced in the first line. Psalm 95:3

➢ Antithetic Parallelism. The Second line contrasts the thought of the first. Psalm 1:6

➢ Emblematic Parallelism. The first line uses a figure of speech to convey the main point which is conveyed explicitly in the second line. Psalm 42:1

➤ Climactic Parallelism. The second line repeats the first line with the exception of the last term. Psalm 29:1

An expanded outline of Hebrew poetry is provided by Bruce Wilkinson in *Talk Thru the Bible*.[8]

Wisdom Literature

The wisdom literature of the Old Testament includes the books of Job, Proverbs and Ecclesiastes. Please note that literary genres are not mutually exclusive and may overlap. The book of Proverbs is both poetry and wisdom literature. The poems of Moses, David, and others are recorded within the historical books.

Wisdom literature includes that genre in which major truths of life and wisdom are addressed or reflected upon.

The Gospels

There is some difference of opinion as to the literary genre of the four Gospels. Some attempt to confine them strictly in the box of ―historical narrative." Some see them as mainly biographical. However, some of us see them containing a variety of genres. Matthew, Mark and Luke are often referred to as the synoptic Gospels because they include many of the same stories, often in the same sequence

---

[8] Bruce Wilkinson, *Talk Thru the Bible*. Nashville: Thomas Nelson Publishers, 1983. pp 140-141

Matthew, Mark, and John, while containing much history and narrative, and thereby qualifying as narrative genre, are primarily doctrinal treatises.

Matthew proves that Jesus of Nazareth is the prophesied Messiah, the rightful King of the Jews, qualified in every way to fulfill the promise of a future King of Israel. This is most clearly seen in the oft repeated phrase, "then was fulfilled what was spoken by the prophet..." Matthew 1:22; 2:5; 2:15; 2:17; 3:3; 4:14; 8:17; 12;17; 13:35; 21:4; 27:9; 27:35.

Mark is unique. Rather than giving a history of the lineage and family history, this Gospel focuses on the works and ministry of Jesus. It presents Jesus as a Savior-King, who conquers demons, disease and death.

The Gospel according to Luke is the only true historical book written on the life and ministry of Jesus. Luke the physician (Col 4:14) wrote this letter as a historian. Luke was not an eye-witness to the events, yet he provides much historical data. He presents Jesus as the Perfect Man Who came to seek and save sinful men. It is the longest and most detailed of the Gospels.

John, "the disciple whom Jesus loved," is the most theological of the four Gospels. Focusing on the divine nature of Christ, John presents Jesus as the Son of God, co-equal with the Father in essence and attributes.

The Gospels, therefore are composed of different literary genres including biographical, historical narrative, and doctrinal.

Logical Discourse

This literary genre is commonly referred to as epistolary literature, and is the primary genre of the New Testament epistles. It might also be referred to as doctrinal discourse. Logical discourse is a written communication addressed or meant for a wide audience that seeks to provoke, induce, or conform behaviors of the audience.

Prophetic Literature

Prophetic Literature is literature which includes predictions of future events, or to put it another way, events that were future at the time of the writing. Some of those events, while future at the time of writing, have since been fulfilled. Others are yet to be fulfilled.

A special part of prophetic literature is *apocalyptic literature*. Apocalyptic literature deals specifically with the end times, which we generally understand to be events from the rapture of the church into the future.

FIGURES OF SPEECH

In addition to the recognition of various literary genres, figures of speech are a major part of rhetorical study. Just as our daily speech is littered and enriched by the use of these figures, so the Bible contains thousands of identifiable and classifiable figures of speech. In this section of our study we will establish a foundation and undertake a study of the figures of speech in Philemon.

A figure of speech is an expression in which the meaning of a word or words is deliberately distorted to render a special literary effect. When interpreting a figure of speech, the normal rules of hermeneutics are retained.

A figure of speech adds interest, vitality, and cultural relevance to speech or to written communication. Since figures of speech are deliberate distortions of normal meaning, they must be self-evident if they are to improve and not impoverish communication.

The seminary that I attended had a very large international population within the student body. It was a great benefit to have the opportunity to meet, worship with, and learn from fellow believers from many different cultures. However, there were times when our cultural differences created comical misunderstandings. Let me share an example. One day between classes a group of us were standing around and talking. We had about a half an hour before the next class and I said in my Texas accent, "I'm so hungry, I could eat a horse." Upon hear me say this one of my fellow students from China excitedly asked, —You eat horse here? I have been craving horse since I got here!"

In the above (true) example, communication failed because it was predicated upon cultural understanding that created a foundation for a figure of speech. It is necessary to understand the culture in order for the figure of speech to become relevant and to prevent misunderstanding.

Tools for the Study of Figures of Speech

Books on Biblical manners and customs will help the student by providing a cultural background against which he or she can recognize figures of speech as they occur. A student of the Word will want these materials in their library.

There is, however, one tool directed to the study of figures of speech as they occur in Scripture. This tool is *Figures of Speech Used in the Bible* by Ethelbert W. Bullinger.[9] This massive work of over 1100 pages includes detailed classifications of figures of speech, five appendices on related subjects, and seven indexes to make the book a suitable tool for reference. These include an index of figures using their proper names, an index of structures, a subject index and indexes of Hebrew and Greek words.

---

[9] E.W. Bullinger, *Figures of Speech Used in the Bible*. Grand Rapids: Baker Book House, 1968

Selected Figures of Speech

Ellipsis	An omission of a word or words in a sentence. Jeremiah 51:19. Note that the ellipsis is supplied by the translators in *italics*.
Meiosis	A diminishing of one thing to increase another. Also called litotes. Romans 10:19; Ephesians 3:8.
Syllogism	Omission of the conclusion, 1 Corinthians 11:6; 2 Thessalonians 3:10.
Parallelism	Synonymous, Antithetic, Synthetic. See previous discussion.
Hermeneia	Interpretation. Hebrews 13:15
Pleonasm	Redundancy. John 5:24; John 1:20
Hyperbole	Exaggeration. Deuteronomy 1:28; Judges 20:16
Metonymy	Change of one noun for a related one. 1 Corinthians 11:26-27
Synecdoche	Change of one idea for another. Part used for the whole. Genesis 14:21; 22:17
Hendiadys	Two words used to mean one thing. Revelation 20:4
Euphemism	Softening. 1 Corinthians 11:30
Simile	Comparison by resemblance using "like" or "as." Psalm 131:2; 1 Peter 1:21
Metaphor	Comparison by resemblance. Isaiah 40:6
Allegory	Continued metaphor. Psalm 23

Type	A figure based on an Old Testament character, event, or institution which, while having reality and purpose in Biblical history, is a divine foreshadowing of things to come. Romans 5:14; 1 Corinthians 5:7
Symbol	A timeless figure of speech in which one item is used to represent another. Revelation 12:9; 20:2
Prosopoeia	Personification. Isaiah 55:12
Anthropomorphism	Condescension. Describing God in human terms. Psalm 71:2; 100:2; John 10:29
Erotasis	Rhetorical question. Asking a question without expecting an answer. 1 Corinthians 12:29-30

This list is by no means exhaustive, but rather it is representative of the figures of speech most used in Scripture.

FIGURES OF SPEECH EXERCISE

1. Read the catalog of figures of speech on the previous pages. Be sure to look up all references and insure that you understand the basic idea of each figure of speech.
2. Read Philemon. Record each figure of speech you find bellow.

Verse   Figure of Speech   Type of Figure

HISTORICAL INTERPRETATION

We now turn our attention to methods of Bible study that emphasize the historical aspects of interpretation. We must remember that the books of the Bible were written by real human authors to real recipients in real time. Now would be a good time to reaffirm our commitment to the literal, historical, grammatical interpretation of God's Word.

How then may we address the historical aspects of Bible study? First, we will observe what may be learned about the human author and the human recipients from the Biblical text itself. We will then examine cultural, geographical, historical, and political data from available sources and will apply the information gleaned to a study of the text.

Upon conclusion of these approaches to study we should find ourselves more nearly "in the shoes" of the original recipient(s) of the book, and thereby better able to understand what Philemon understood when he received this epistle from the hand of the Apostle Paul.

Author / Recipient Study

The Author / Recipient study is a focused form of observation and interpretation in which we center our study on the human persons of the author and the recipient(s) of a particular book of the Bible. First, we make observations from the Biblical text and then interpret the information we have learned by writing a short paper on the human author, followed by another on the person of the human recipient(s) on the book being studied.

Following, you will find the text of Philemon with wide margins on either side of the text. Read the text and record the information disclosed about the human author in the left margin. Then record information about the human recipient, Philemon, in the right margin. You may find it helpful to read the text several times, in order to be comprehensive in your study.

Once you have completed taking notes about the author and the recipients, write a short paper describing the human author as you have come to know him through this book.

Author / Recipient Study in Philemon

AUTHOR		RECIPIENT
	Paul, a prisoner of Christ Jesus, and Timothy our brother, To Philemon our beloved friend and fellow laborer, to the beloved Apphia, Archippus our fellow soldier, and to the church in your house: Grace to you and peace from God our Father and the Lord Jesus Christ. I thank my God, making mention of you always in my prayers, hearing of your love and faith which	

you have toward the Lord Jesus and toward all the saints, that the sharing of your faith may become effective by the acknowledgment of every good thing which is in you in Christ Jesus. For we have great joy and consolation in your love, because the hearts of the saints have been refreshed by you, brother. Therefore, though I might be very bold in Christ to command you what is fitting, yet for love's sake I rather appeal to you--being such a one as Paul, the aged, and now also a prisoner of Jesus Christ-- I appeal to you for my son Onesimus, whom I have begotten while in my chains, who once was unprofitable to you, but now is profitable to you and to me. I am sending him back. You therefore receive him, that is, my own heart, whom I wished to keep with me, that on your behalf he might minister to me in my chains for the gospel. But without your consent I wanted to do nothing, that your good deed might not be by compulsion, as it were, but voluntary. For perhaps he departed for a while for this purpose, that you might receive him forever, no longer as a slave but more than a slave--a beloved brother, especially to me but how much more to you, both in the flesh and in the Lord. If then you count me as a partner, receive him as you would me. But if he has wronged you or owes anything, put that on my account. I, Paul, am writing with my own hand. I will repay--not to mention to you that you owe me even your own self besides. Yes, brother, let me have joy from you in the Lord; refresh my heart in the Lord. Having confidence in your obedience, I write to you, knowing that you will do even more than I say. But, meanwhile, also prepare a guest room for me, for I trust that through your prayers I shall be granted to you. Epaphras, my fellow prisoner in Christ Jesus, greets you, as do Mark,

> Aristarchus, Demas, Luke, my fellow laborers. The grace of our Lord Jesus Christ be with your spirit. Amen.

THE HUMAN AUTHOR OF PHILEMON

Use this space to write your summary about the human author of Philemon. Please keep in mind, that this is to be a summary, not a biography. Include only those facts that you can ascertain from the text of Philemon itself. This should be done in no more than two or three paragraphs.

THE RECIPIENT OF PHILEMON

Use this space to write your summary of the recipient of Philemon. Please keep in mind, that this is to be a summary, not a biography. Include only those facts that you can ascertain from the text of Philemon itself. This should be done in no more than two or three paragraphs.

CULTURAL STUDY

If we are to understand the epistle to Philemon as it was understood by the original recipient, we must place ourselves into the same framework of understanding that was experienced by Philemon and his family. We must understand that we do not live in the same culture. Therefore, we must learn to read Scripture through cross-cultural lenses.

To become culturally sensitive to the mores of the New Testament, we will need to do outside reading and research. There are a large number of tools which can help us at this point of our study.

Tools for Cultural Study

One of the most valuable types of tool for cultural study is a good book on manners and customs. They are specifically designed to help the student to mentally place themselves into the New Testament culture. Many of them point out and address specific Scripture verses which have cultural nuances different from our own. They are easy to use and relatively inexpensive to buy.

My favorite of all of these cultural study tools is *The New Manners and Customs of Bible Times*, by Ralph Gower. This book is divided into two sections, "The individual in Family Life" and "National Institutions and Customs."

Another helpful volume for cultural study is *Nelson's New Illustrated Bible Manners & Customs*. This work is arranged by Bible periods beginning with Abraham in Genesis 11 and moving through

Rome during the time of the Apostle Paul's career as seen in Acts 28.

A third book that will be found helpful for cultural study is the *Dictionary of Paul and his Letters*. Though this volume is more academic, it is none the less a great tool for cultural discovery.

Identifying Texts for Cultural Study

How does the student know what texts require cultural study? There are two simple ways. First, read through the book of Philemon and make a list of subjects that have the appearance being culturally oriented. You will recognize some things in the text that stand out as being part of a culture different than yours.

The second method is to use one of the resource tools for the study of Bible manners and customs. Use the Scripture index and look up the book of Philemon. See what the author has identified as a culturally relevant subject for study.

Conducting a Cultural Study

Once the student has identified possible subjects for cultural study he is ready to begin the study. Using tools for cultural study, research each subject, learning all that you can about how this subject was understood and dealt with during the time of the writing. Then write a brief report on what you have learned.

Exercise for Cultural Study

There are several possible subjects of a cultural nature found in Philemon which could be profitably studied. Since the subject of slavery is foundational to the study of Philemon we will focus on this subject for cultural study. Using whatever tools that are available to you (the more the better), study New Testament slavery as pictured in Philemon. Write a brief 3-5 page report of what you have learned. Be sure to identify the sources used.

GEOGRAPHICAL STUDY

Another important kind of background study is geographical study. The careful Bible student will want to identify all of the places he reads about in Scripture. These may include named places, called *political* references and features of the land called *physical* references. The study of these two kinds of references is called political geography and physical geography.

Tools for Geographical Study

The primary tool for geographical Bible study is a Bible atlas. Many are available to suit the taste and needs of individual students. Most personal study Bibles contain maps and a brief index. More complete maps and indexes are included in Bible atlases. The following are recommended:

The Moody Atlas of Bible Lands by Barry Beitzel is this author's favorite offering. The text and maps are clear and accurate. The maps are full color, attractive, and easy to read. The map citation index and Scripture index are great reference tools.

The MacMillan Bible Atlas is particularly useful for the study of the Old Testament historical books. This atlas uses "mini-maps" in which it explains each aspect of the Old Testament battles. This unique contribution makes it worth having as a geographical tool.

The "Logos Bible Atlas[10]" is Bible atlas software. This format is excellent for those who wish to conduct

---

[10] "Logos Bible Atlas," Oak Harbor, WA; Logos Software, 1996

electronic searches and produce color printed maps for use in Bible study.

The *Holman Book of Biblical Charts, Maps and Reconstructions* is an excellent resource, a collection of many helpful Bible tools. The reconstructions are clear and vivid and the color maps are outstanding.

Conducting a Geographical Study

Performing a geographical study involves discovering geographical references in the text being studied, looking them up in a Bible atlas and noting any important or interesting information gleaned.

In some cases, such as our study of Philemon there are no explicit mentions of geographical places. Nevertheless, there is implied geography. Where was Paul when he wrote the letter? Where was Philemon? These "where" questions need to be asked and answered for our Bible studies.

Exercise for Geographical Study

Read Philemon in one sitting. List each reference to a place or other geographical feature. Indicate the chapter and verse following the name of the place or feature. As previously discussed, some books do not mention any specific places by name, but they do refer to some places. For instance, from where did Paul write? In which city did Philemon live? Where did the church meet? (Hint: Compare Philemon 2, 12 with Colossians 4:9, 17).

Place or Feature   Bible Reference

HISTORICAL STUDY

By the general term historical study, we mean that study which helps us to identify the historical background of a Bible book. We have touched on this broad area already in learning to do cultural and biographical studies. At this point we will probe further into the historical background that underlies a Bible book.

It is good to remember here that as we interpret the Bible we seek to put ourselves into the interpretive shoes of the original recipients of the Scripture being studied. By better understanding what those original recipients would have understood, we have the best opportunity to discover the intent of the human author of the book.

It is to this purpose that historical study commends itself. Through good historical study we make a deliberate, conscious shift into the culture, geography, political, and historical setting of the original recipients.

Historical study of this kind is necessarily broad and is greatly dependent upon the Bible book being studied. The historical background of the book of Acts, for example, is obvious and extensive. Everything about Roman rule in the days of the first century church becomes relevant to the study. The books of the Old Testament have similar and extensive historical backgrounds.

When interpreting the New Testament epistles, remember that these do fit in the time-space continuum of the book of Acts, however, they often deal with matters that are more theological than historical. A casual reading of Philemon is not likely to send us scampering for deeper historical data. Yet, the student will soon discover the need for further historical research to enhance our understanding of this book.

In Philemon verse two Paul refers to the church that evidently met in the home of Philemon. That could be considered and important cultural element in our study. It might also be considered a matter of the history of the early Christian church and studied as a phenomenon of historical development. More to the point, every paragraph of Sacred Scripture has its place in the historical record. The more that the student discovers about that record, the better equipped he or she will be to properly interpret it.

In this section we will introduce some of the tools that you will find helpful in further historical study.

Bible Dictionaries

A good Bible dictionary is an absolute essential tool in any Bible student's library. Of all of the Bible dictionaries that I have reviewed I am most impressed with the *New Unger's Bible Dictionary*. It contains articles on each book of the Bible, and thereby provides some limited historical background.

Bible Encyclopedias

Bible Encyclopedias are generally multi-volume tools with more extensive information and longer articles than dictionaries. They generally provide more depth into historical backgrounds and are therefore essential to do deep background studies.

Bible Introduction

Bible Introductions approach the Bible book by book, answering historical questions dealing with authorship, date, sources, purpose, destination, and the like.

Church History

There are some church history works that specifically address the church in the first century, and these usually discuss the historical backgrounds of the epistles. For the study of the Old Testament, you will find many works on the history of Israel.

Approaching Historical Study

Your approach to historical study will vary based on the Biblical genre being studied. For instance when studying a historical narrative, you will find yourself researching the political, cultural climate in which the recipients lived. When studying the wisdom literature or the epistles, you may direct your historical research toward specific problems being addressed or the philosophical temperament of the time.

As we begin our historical study for Philemon, start by reading a brief article in a good conservative Bible introduction. This will assist you in narrowing down the date, place, and general background of the book.

Historical Study Exercise

Let us focus our study and thereby more clearly define our subject. Paul wrote the epistle to Philemon from prison. Our focus for this Exercise is to discover what we can about imprisonment during the first century, and the imprisonment of Paul in particular.

Having begun in a general Bible introduction we have identified the general background of the book. Now let us move to Bible dictionaries and encyclopedias to learn more about imprisonment at the time Philemon was written.

When you have gathered sufficient information write a brief (2-3 pages) paper on the subject of Roman imprisonment in the first century.

GRAMMATICAL ANALYSIS

Grammatical study is that study which emphasizes the grammar found in the word of the Biblical text. Webster defines grammar as "the study of the way the sentences of a language are constructed... the study of morphology and syntax.[11]" Whenever we study the Bible we must do so with the understanding that it was not originally written in English. There are a variety of language tools available to the non-language student.

When doing a thorough study of a Biblical text, paying particular attention to the grammar and syntax as found in the original language, we call it *exegesis*. Exegetical study is one of the most labor intensive elements of personal Bible study however, the benefits of this discipline far outweigh any apprehension. In order to be able to properly exegete the text the non-language student must become competent in two arts. First, the student must learn to properly use the appropriate language tools available. Second, the student must become proficient in the rules and usage of English grammar.

It was recently remarked that of the recent admittees to a leading West Coast seminary only four students were able to pass the Basic English exam! This fact was despite that the majority were English speaking students.

While this is not an English grammar course of study, it is important for a Bible student to know the basics of grammar to properly interpret the Bible.

---

[11] Webster's American Dictionary, College Edition. New York: Random House, 1997.

Therefore, let us conduct a brief review of English grammar before moving on to the procedures and benefits of the grammatical chart.

It is recommended that the student procure an English grammar handbook. This can be used in Bible study, in composition and in general communication. I still use the *Webster's New World English Grammar Handbook*[12] by Kate Shoup that I purchased in a used bookstore 15 years ago. It is not a fancy book, but it helps keep me on the right track.

REVIEWING ENGLISH GRAMMAR
Parts of Speech
We begin with the words themselves. Each word in English belongs to a *part of speech*, which describes how it is used. These must be mastered.

Noun—The name of a person, place, thing or idea.

Pronoun—A word that takes the place of a noun and refers back to it.

Verb—A word of action or state of being.

Adjective—A word that describes a noun or a pronoun.

Adverb—a word that describes a verb, and adjective, or another adverb.

---

[12] Kate Shoup, *Webster's New World English Grammar Handbook Second Edition*. New York: Wiley, 2009

Preposition—A word that shows the relation between a noun or pronoun and some other word in the sentence.

Conjunction—A word which joins words or groups of words.

Interjection—A word that expresses emotion and has no grammatical relation to the other words in the sentence.

All words in English act as one or more of these parts of speech. Some words will act as more than one part of speech in different uses. The word "park" may be a noun when it names a piece of land with trees and grass and play equipment. It may also be a verb when it is used of one putting a car into a position of short term rest. Therefore we conclude that a part of speech comes from the way a word is used in a sentence or its context.

Groups of Words
Words do not generally stand alone but occur in meaningful groups.

Phrase—A group of related words.

Clause—A group of related words with a subject and a predicate (verb).

Sentence—A group of related words with a subject and a predicate that is able to stand alone and which expresses a complete though.

Paragraph—A group of related sentences which discuss some topic. The topic is generally introduced in the first sentence in the paragraph and is usually referred to as the topic sentence.

Kinds of Sentences

Sentences in English are one of four kinds:

Declarative—A sentence which makes a statement. It is ended with a period.

Interrogative—A sentence which asks a question. It ends with a question mark.

Imperative—A sentence that gives a command. It is ended with either a period or an exclamation mark.

Exclamatory—A sentence that shows strong emotion. It is ended with an exclamation mark.

The Parts of a Sentence

A sentence consists of two major parts: the subject and the predicate. The subject of the sentence tells what is being discussed. The predicate tells what happens to the subject.

Simple Subject— The single word about which the sentence is written is called the **simple subject.** It must be a noun, a pronoun, or a group of words acting as a noun.

Simple Predicate— The single word which tells what the subject is or does is called the **simple predicate**. The simple predicate must be a verb or a verbal. The verb may have another verb called a helping verb to show tense.

Compound Subject— A **compound subject** is two or more connected nouns or pronouns which tell together who or what is being discussed in the sentence.

Compound Predicate— A **compound predicate** is two or more verbs which tell what happens to the subject.

SENTENCE ANALYSIS

When analyzing a sentence always begin with the simple predicate. To find the simple predicate ask —What action or state of being is affirmed here?" The single word that shows an action or state of being is the simple predicate. As stated before the simple predicate may have a helping verb to show tense, we will discuss that later.

When you discover the simple predicate it is time to discover the simple subject. Asked the question "Who or what carries out the action of the simple predicate?" Or "Who or what is said to exist in this sentence?" The answer is the simple subject. If this sentence is an imperative sentence, a command, the subject is nearly always understood but not mentioned. The subject is "you." In the sentence *take out the trash* the subject is understood. The sentence means *you take out the trash*. In the case of interrogative sentence (a question), turn the sentence around to find the subject. *Where is the book*? Becomes *the book is where*? For the purpose of discovering the simple subject. Now you ask the question "what is being spoken about" and the answer is "the book."

You can quickly see that word order is important in English. It is the word order that determines who the subject is. That is not so in Greek, the original language of the New Testament. In Greek each word has an ending to show the reader how it is being used in the sentence.

Complements

Some sentences express a complete thought with just a subject and a verb. *She fell* and *God exists* are examples of this kind of sentence. But most sentences have a third key part that completes the thought of the sentence. These are called complements. There are two basic kinds.

1. A complement that completes the thought in a sentence with an action verb is called an object complement. There are two kinds of object complements.
    - A noun or pronoun in the predicate that receives the action of an action verb is called the *direct object*.
    - A noun or pronoun in the predicate receiving the direct object and telling to whom or for whom the action takes place is called the *indirect object*.
2. A complement that completes the thought in a sentence with a state of being verb is called the subject complement. There are two types of subject complements.
    - A noun or pronoun in the predicate following a state of being verb referring back to the subject is called a *predicate nominative*.
    - An adjective in the predicate, following a state of being verb describing the subject is called a *predicate adjective*.

Sentence Analysis

The three major parts of most sentences are subject, verb, and complement. When we analyze the sentence we start with a verb. Is it in action or state of being verb? Then we move to the subject. Who is doing the action or to whom does the state of being referrer? Then we search for the complement. Who or what receives the action of the verb? Or, if it is a state of being verb, is there a noun or pronoun in the predicate refers back to the subject? Or is there an adjective in the predicate that describes the subject? These are the three major parts of any English sentence. The other words expand upon or describe these three major sentence parts.

Phrases

A phrase is a group of related words. Phrases in English generally act as if they were one word. That is, a prepositional phrase may act as a noun, an adjective, or an adverb. An infinitive phrase acts like a noun. A participial phrase acts like an adjective. A gerund phrase acts like a noun. Let's examine these phrases.

Prepositional Phrases.

A preposition is a word that connects a noun or pronoun, called the object of the preposition, with the rest of the sentence and shows the relationship between them. We generally learn to recognize common prepositional phrases in English. The following words are commonly used as prepositions:

about, above, across, after, against, along, among, around, at, before, behind, below, beneath, beside, besides, between, beyond, by, concerning, down, during, except, for, from, in, into, like, of, off, on, over, past, since, through, throughout, to, toward, under, underneath, until, unto, up, upon, with, within, without.

Notice that these words tend to show physical (spatial) relationships or temporal (time) relationships. That is, they tend to answer the questions where or when.

A prepositional phrase consists of a preposition followed by a noun or pronoun which is its object. It will frequently have one or more adjectives in the phrase. The following are prepositional phrases:

on the swing, under the house, over my dresser, in the big tree, concerning your job, by the riverbank, between the streets, after the party, against my better judgment, among the believers, at the church picnic.

Each prepositional phrase above has a **preposition**, a word which shows relationship, followed by a noun which is its **object**. Before the noun is one or more **adjectives** which describe the noun. The word "the" is a special kind of adjective called an **article**. Together these words make up prepositional phrases.

Prepositional phrases generally act as modifiers in the sentence. That is, they describe nouns or pronouns or they describe verbs, adjectives, or adverbs. The entire prepositional phrase acts like an adjective when it describes a noun or pronoun. (Remember adjectives are words which describe nouns or pronouns). When the prepositional phrase describes a verb, adjective, or adverb it acts like an adverb. (Adverbs are words which describe verbs, adjectives, or other adverbs). Therefore, we say the prepositional phrases are either adjectival phrases or adverbial phrases.

Verbal Phrases

A verbal is a word formed from a verb that functions as another part of speech. A **participial** is a verbal which is formed from a verb but acts like an adjective. In this sentence, "*the singing choir marched onto the platform*" the word *singing* which describes the choir must be an adjective. It is made up from a verb (the verb to sing) but in this sentence it is describing the *choir*. Since *choir* is a noun the word singing which describes it must be an adjective remember that parts of speech are determined by the function a word has in a sentence.

We can add other words to a participle to make it a participial phrase. Suppose we expand our sentence to, "*the joyfully singing choir marched onto the platform.*" The words *joyfully singing* are a participial phrase describing the choir, used as an adjective in the sentence.

Gerund

A gerund is a word formed from a verb which functions as a noun and a verb at the same time. The word generally ends in -ing. In the sentence, "*teaching is important*" the word *teaching* is a gerund. It comes from the verb to teach but is functioning as a noun in the sentence.

When we add additional words to a gerund we form a gerund phrase. Suppose we said, "*Teaching the Bible is important.*" The words *teaching the Bible* constitute a gerund phrase. The gerund acts as a subject in this sentence. But notice that *Bible* receives the action of being taught. It is the object of the gerund teaching. The gerund functions as both a noun and a verb. As a noun *teaching* is the subject of the sentence. As a verb teaching takes an object complement, *Bible*.

Appositives

An appositive is a noun or pronoun that follows another noun or pronoun to explain it. The appositive often includes modifiers. When it includes other words it is called an appositive phrase. Consider the sentence, "Alpha, our overweight kitty cat, believes every visitor that comes to our home has come to play with her." The subject of the sentence is *Alpha*. The phrase *our overweight kitty cat* is in apposition to Alpha. The word *cat* is the appositive, a noun that further explains the noun Alpha. The words *our overweight kitty* are adjectives that describe the cat. Taken together, the words *our overweight kitty cat* are an appositive phrase.

In the same sentence the words *to play* are an infinitive telling why a visitor comes. *To play with her* forms an infinitive phrase (a phrase with an infinitive in it). The words *with her* are prepositional phrase used as an adverb telling how a visitor plays. We use many phrases in our everyday English speech!

Sentence Analysis

It is helpful for the student to form systematic habits when analyzing sentences. First, find the verb, then the subject, then the complement. Look at each word to determine its part of speech. Then determine its use in the sentence. Suppose I were analyzing John 1:1. I would write out the text leaving room between the lines.

In the beginning was the Word,

and the Word was with God,

and the Word was God.

I would select a first sentence beginning with *in* and ending with *God*. The first thing that I want to find is the verb, the simple predicate. I look for a word that shows action or state of being in the sentence. I see the word *was* and recognize that it is a state of being verb. I print the letter "V" over the word to show me that it is a verb. Over the "V" I print "pred" for predicate, reminding me that this is the verb for the sentence. Then I ask the question, who or what *was* something in the sentence? The answer is that the

Word was. On top of *word* I print an "n" for noun over the "n" I write "subj" for subject. I next look for a complement. Since the verb is a state of being rather than an action verb there could be a subject complement, but there could not be an object complement. A subject complement is a noun, pronoun, or adjective in the predicate that refers back to the subject. I asked, "is there a noun, pronoun or adjective that refers back to *Word*? I don't find one, so I conclude that there is no subject complement in this sentence.

I now begin to work through the remaining words. *The* is a word describing *Word*, so I write "adj" (for adjective) over it and draw an arrow to *Word*, the word it describes. I recognize that *in* is on the preposition list. I write "prep" (for preposition) over *in*. *Beginning* is a noun (the name of a person, place, thing, or idea) so I put "n" for noun over *beginning*. *Beginning* must be the object of the preposition in, so I write "oop" for object of preposition over the "n" over the word *beginning*. The word *the* acts as an adjective, explaining which beginning we are speaking of. Therefore, I write "adj" over *the* and draw an arrow to the word *beginning*. What does the prepositional phrase *in the beginning* do in this sentence? It tells us about the *Word*. So I draw an arrow from *in* to *Word*.

I'm on a roll here! I move on to the phrase "and the Word was with God." Sticking to my system, I notice that there is a verb *was*. As you may have guessed, this is a verb of being, therefore I treat the same as last time. After analyzing my verb, I look for my subject... *Word*. Again, we see the word *the* operating as an adjective describing the word *Word*.

I recognize that there is another prepositional phrase here, *with God*. The word *with* being a preposition, the word *God* being the object of the preposition.

Looking at the last phrase of this verse, I again locate my verb *was*. Then the subject, *Word*. And now we come to something different. Notice the word *God*, the verb of being *was* equates the *Word* to *God*. This is an appositive.

Once I have finished this exercise, my worksheet now looks like this:

Prep	adj	opp	v (pred)	adj	n (sub)
In	the	beginning	was	the	Word,

Conj	adj	n (sub)	v (pred)	prep	opp
and	the	Word	was	with	God,

Conj	adj	n (suj)	v (pred)	app
and	the	Word	was	God.

We finished the sentence. Did that seem difficult? Many English readers are not very good in English grammar, but the more you do it the easier it will become. It is important to remember, **if we do not know what a word is doing in the sentence then how we know how to interpret the Bible verse?** It is imperative that we learn to do grammatical analysis in whatever language we are studying. If you'd rather do this in the original language, Greek, that is even better. But until you learn the rules of Greek grammar and syntax you'll need to do it in English.

Practice

It is now your turn. On the following Grammatical Analysis Worksheet you will analyze each word in Philemon verses one and two. You may look back at your notebook or at an English grammar handbook as often as necessary. If you keep doing this kind of analysis it will become almost automatic and you won't need to use a handbook or your notes as often to look things up.

Grammatical Analysis Worksheet
Philemon 1-2

Paul, a prisoner of Christ Jesus, and Timothy our brother,

To Philemon our beloved friend and fellow laborer,

to the beloved Apphia, Archippus our fellow soldier,

and to the church in your house:

Clauses

A clause is a group of related words with the subject and predicate. There are two major kinds of clauses, independent and dependent. An **independent clause** is able to stand alone grammatically. A **dependent clause** is not able to stand alone; it depends on an independent clause to support it. Dependent clauses are sometimes called **subordinate clauses**. Subordinate clauses are used as nouns, adjectives, or adverbs. The entire clause has the same function as a noun, adjective or adverb.

An adjective clause is a subordinate clause which like an adjective, describes a noun or pronoun. Consider the sentence, *"the book that you gave me was helpful in my studies."* The words, *"that you gave me"* is a subordinate clause. It has a subject (you) and a verb (gave). The entire clause describes *book*. Since the word *book* is a noun, the clause *"that you gave me"* is an adjective clause.

Consider this sentence, *"I'm thankful to God for believers who helped me."* The words, *"who helped me"* form a subordinate clause. The clause *"who helped me"* describes *believers*. Since *believers* is a noun the clause must be an adjective clause because words and clauses that describe nouns are adjectives.

Notice that the adjective clauses in these sentences are joined to the rest of the sentence with a connecting word. These words are called **relative pronouns**. Relative pronouns include the words *who, whom, whose, which, what,* and *that.* Relative (or demonstrative) pronouns relate the subordinate clause to a word in an independent clause.

A **noun clause** is a subordinate clause used as a noun. Like a noun, it may be the subject of the sentence, a direct object, or the object of a preposition. Consider these sentences:

1. I remember the sermon.

2. I remember what was preached.

In sentence number one the *sermon* is the direct object. It receives the action of being remembered. In sentence number two, *what was preached* functions in the same way. But *what was preached* is a clause with a subject (what) and verb (was preached). The words, *"what was preached"* is a noun clause.

Consider these sentences:

1. Eternal life is given to believers.

2. Eternal life is given to whomever believes.

In sentence one, *believers* is the object of the preposition *to*. In sentence two, *whomever believes* functions in the same way. The words *whomever believes* is a clause with a subject (whomever) and a verb (believes).

An **adverb clause** is a subordinate clause that functions like an adverb. Remember that an adverb describes a verb, an adjective, or another adverb. Frequently adverbs, and adverb clauses, tell how, when, where, why, to what extent, and under what conditions.

See if you can locate the adverb clauses in the following sentences.

1. He prays as if his life depended on it.
2. He prays whenever he can.
3. She prays everywhere she goes.
4. She prays because God told her to in the Bible.
5. He prays as long as he can.
6. She prays if she thinks about it.

Each of these sentences has an adverb clause which tell in order, *how, when, where, why, to what extent,* and *under what conditions.* In each sentence the adverb clause describes the word *prays*, the verb.

In his writings, the apostle Paul is especially fond of joining many subordinate clauses together to make an extraordinarily long sentence. While these appear to be complex, they can be simplified by treating one clause of the time.

At this time we will continue our grammatical analysis of Philemon using the worksheet provided on the following page.

Grammatical Analysis Worksheet
Philemon 3-6

Grace to you and peace from God our Father and the Lord Jesus Christ. I thank my God, making mention of you always in my prayers, hearing of your love and faith which you have toward the Lord Jesus and toward all the saints, that the sharing of your faith may become effective by the acknowledgment of every good thing which is in you in Christ Jesus.

More About Verbs

Every verb has five important characteristics. These are person, number, tense, voice, and mood.

Person is the relation between the speaker or writer and the subject of the sentence. In the **first person**, the speaker or writer and the subject are the same. The personal pronoun that best represents this is "I" or "we." In the **second person,** the speaker or writer refers to the one or ones to whom he or she is speaking. The personal pronoun which best expresses this is "you." In the **third person**, the speaker or writer refers to anything or to anyone other than the speaker or the one or ones being addressed. The personal pronouns that best expresses relationship are "he, she, it," and "they." These persons are reflected in the form of English verbs. Consider the following conjugation of the verb "go."

	Singular	*Plural*
1st person	I go	We go
2nd person	You go	You go
3rd person	He, she, it goes	They go

The second important factor about verbs is number. **Number** is used to indicate whether a word has one or more than one referent, referred to by the terms singular or plural. You'll notice in the paradigm above we have separate columns for singular and plural.

A third important factor in verbs is their tense. **Tense** is the relationship between the verb and time. In basic English there are three tenses of a verb.

1. The **present tense** shows something happening at the present time. *You are now reading this page.*
2. The **past tense** shows something happening in past time. Sometimes the helping verbs "was" or "did" may occur in this form. *You did buy this book.*
3. The **future tense** shows something that will happen in the future. The future tense uses the helping verb "will" or "shall." *You will do the next Exercise.*

NOTE: There are other variations of the basic three tenses in the English language. However that is far more advanced that we are going to be getting in this volume.

The next important characteristic about a verb is its **voice**. The voice of a verb shows the relationship between the subject and the action. In English grammar there are only two voices, active, and passive. In the active voice the subject performs the action of the verb. In the passive voice the subject receives the action of the verb.

1. Active- "The boy hit the ball."

2. Passive- "The ball was hit by the boy."

In sentence number one, which is in the active voice the subject performs the action of the verb. In sentence number two, the subject receives the action of the verb.

The fifth characteristic is **mood**. Mood shows the relationship between the verb in reality. There are three moods in English, the indicative, the imperative, and the subjunctive.

The **indicative mood** is the mood of reality. If the verb occurs in the indicative mood, the action is really taking place (or did really take place, or really will take place). "I am going to the store." "I was in a meeting."

The **imperative mood** is the mood of command. The action is not true now, but is expected to become true. This is sometimes called the mood of necessity. "Go to the store." "Go therefore and make disciples…"

The **subjunctive mood** is the mood of non-reality. It either expresses something that is contrary to fact or something that is being wished for. "I should go to the store." "I might go to the store." "I ought to go to the store."

Every English verb expresses person, number, tense, voice, and mood.

It is now time to continue with our grammatical analysis of Philemon. Please use the worksheet provided on the following page.

Grammatical Analysis Worksheet
Philemon 7-11

For we have great joy and consolation in your love, because the hearts of the saints have been refreshed by you, brother. Therefore, though I might be very bold in Christ to command you what is fitting, yet for love's sake I rather appeal to you--being such a one as Paul, the aged, and now also a prisoner of Jesus Christ-- I appeal to you for my son Onesimus, whom I have begotten while in my chains, who once was unprofitable to you, but now is profitable to you and to me.

More About Nouns

Nouns in English express gender, number, in case.

Gender is a grammatical term that is often confused with sexuality. Gender is masculine, feminine, or neuter. It is true that male persons in English are referred to in the masculine and female persons in the feminine. But there in inanimate objects, like ships, that are by custom referred to as feminine. These are represented by the personal pronouns, "he, she, and it," respectively.

Number for nouns is the same as number for verbs. Singular means only one, while plural means more than one.

Case indicates the way a noun or pronoun is used in the sentence. There are four cases in English, the subjective, possessive, objective, and the case of direct address. Only the possessive case has a distinctive form. The other cases use the same form of the word and are determined by context, punctuation, or other helping words.

	Singular	*Plural*
Subjective	Boy	Boys
Possessive	Boy's	Boys'
Objective	Boy	Boys
Direct address	Boy!	Boys!

Please complete the grammatical analysis of Philemon using the worksheet on the following pages.

Grammatical Analysis Worksheet
Philemon 12-25

I am sending him back. You therefore receive him,

that is, my own heart, whom I wished to keep with

me, that on your behalf he might minister to me in my

chains for the gospel. But without your consent I

wanted to do nothing, that your good deed might not

be by compulsion, as it were, but voluntary. For

perhaps he departed for a while for this purpose, that

you might receive him forever, no longer as a slave

but more than a slave--a beloved brother, especially to

me but how much more to you, both in the flesh and

in the Lord. If then you count me as a partner, receive him as you would me. But if he has wronged you or owes anything, put that on my account. I, Paul, am writing with my own hand. I will repay--not to mention to you that you owe me even your own self besides. Yes, brother, let me have joy from you in the Lord; refresh my heart in the Lord. Having confidence in your obedience, I write to you, knowing that you will do even more than I say. But, meanwhile, also prepare a guest room for me, for I trust that through your prayers I shall be granted to you. Epaphras, my fellow prisoner in Christ Jesus, greets you, as do Mark, Aristarchus, Demas, Luke, my fellow laborers.

The grace of our Lord Jesus Christ be with your spirit.

Amen.

The Grammatical Structure Chart

A grammatical structure chart, sometimes called a mechanical chart, is a useful tool for reviewing an entire book of the Bible based on grammatical function. The chart is simple to make after the student has done the grammatical analysis. On a sheet of paper make three imaginary columns by writing headings but not drawing lines. The three column headings are subject, verb, and complements. You may choose to write in modifiers under the subject, verb, and complement. You may choose to make your chart uncluttered by omitting descriptors. Work your way through the book listing each subject, verb, and complement. When you are done you will have all the subjects in one column all the verbs in another and all the complements the third. This gives you an instant picture of the grammatical development of the book.

Chapter Four
THE SKILL OF CORRELATION

We have now completed the Observation and Interpretation phases of our inductive Bible study. The next major aspect of our study is Correlation.

Observation answered the question, "What does it say?" Interpretation answered the question, "What does it mean?" Correlation will answer the question, "What do other passages of Scripture say about the same subject?"

In this section we will learn three methods of Bible study that answer this question, methods that address the whole of Sacred Scripture as it applies to the book of Philemon.

The Biographical Method

The biographical method of study is one in which we study what the Scripture tells us about some person mentioned in the Bible book we are studying. It is easy for students to read over lists of names without paying much attention to the lives that are represented. As one young student put it, "they are all unpronounceable names from faraway places." In this study we pause to reflect on who these people are.

The book of Philemon mentions a cluster of important persons. This list includes: Paul, Timothy, Philemon, Apphia, Archippus, Onesimus, Epaphras, Aristarchus, Demas, and Luke. Notice that there are 11 people mentioned in a book of only 25 verses.

How to Do the Study

Inasmuch as these appear to be New Testament characters, the simplest way to conduct the study is to use a concordance. Let's consider the Strong's concordance. Dr. James Strong scoured through the entire Bible and he wrote down every Hebrew and Greek word that underlie an English word. He then put the Hebrew words in alphabetical order in Hebrew, and he numbered them. He did the same for Greek, putting all the New Testament words in alphabetical order in Greek and numbering them as well. The result is that the English Bible student can access the Hebrew and Greek words by number without knowing a single letter of the Greek or Hebrew alphabet.

Another phenomenal tool for doing this type of study is the *Word Study Concordance and New Testament.* Using volume 1 of this two volume set you look for the book of Philemon. It starts on page 690. As you begin to read Philemon you'll notice the Strong's numbers beneath each keyword. As you read through the book of Philemon in one column write down every proper name that you come across. Then in a second column, right down the Strong's number that appears by that name.

Once you've completed this take volume 2 of the set, which is the concordance. In this volume, look up each Strong's number that you have annotated.

Once you've located the Strong's number, the concordance will list every verse in which that word appears in the Greek New Testament. You can then systematically look up every occurrence of that word or name in the New Testament. As you do this you will discover that you have learned more and more about the individual who you are studying.

Word Studies

One most valuable kinds of Bible study is the word study. This is an important study because we understand that the very words of Scripture are inspired by God. The Holy Spirit supernaturally compared God's revelation with the vocabularies and literary styles of the human authors so that the human authors of Scripture wrote exactly what God wanted written using their own individual personalities and styles. This is explained for us in 1 Corinthians 2:13.

> These things which we speak, not in words which man's wisdom teaches but which the Holy Spirit teaches, comparing spiritual things with spiritual.
> -1 Corinthians 2:13.

The same concept is also explained in 2 Peter 1:21.

> Holy men of God spoke as they were moved by the Holy Spirit.
> -2 Peter 1:21

This is why we believe it is so important to study the actual words of Scripture and to study them in the original languages in which they were given. As we have already learned, we are able to do Greek New Testament word studies even though we may not know a single letter of the Greek alphabet. This exercise will take you step-by-step through Greek word studies. Before we begin the actual study, it will help us to consider some of the principles that grow out of our hermeneutics.

Some Basic Principles

Words always gain their meaning from context. When we think of the English word "post" we immediately realized that it is capable of several meanings. Whether it is referring to a place where the Army lives, a breakfast cereal, a stake that you hang a fence or sign on, r a position within the company, will be clearly indicated by the context in which the word is used. Therefore, we must study words in their context.

Based on 1 Corinthians 2:13 and 2 Peter 1:21 we know that the choice of words in the original languages of the Bible is deliberate and not incidental to the meaning of the text. Therefore it is of the utmost importance that we study words in their original languages, even if we do not know how to read those languages ourselves.

When Scripture is translated from one language to another there is a tendency to obscure the meaning of words. Different languages use words differently. It is unlikely that any language other than English has the same set of possible meanings for the word "post." In Spanish, there are separate words for "I am *hot*," "the water is *hot*," and "the food is *hot*." But, in English they are all translated "hot." This is the primary reason why it is preferable to do word studies in the original languages.

Since God deliberately chose the words that would be used in Scripture we conclude that different words generally have different meanings unless clearly equated by usage. We do not assume that different Greek words have the same meaning just because they might be translated the same English word.

With these principles fresh in our minds let's begin.

Tools for Word Studies

There are several different tools that can be used to do a word study in Scripture. These include: *Strong's Concordance, Young's Analytical Concordance to the Bible*, and *The Word Study New Testament and Concordance*. In addition there are several computer programs available that will aid you in your search for words in the original language. One excellent tool can be found at www.Biblestudytools.com under the interlinear section.

In this study we will use the *Word Study New Testament and Concordance*. Each of the tool cited above all have one thing in common, they are used to locate the occurrences of words in the Bible in their original languages.

How to Do Word Studies

Suppose you're reading 2 Timothy and you notice the word "endure" in 2 Timothy 2:10. You want to know what it means to "endure." The solution to this question is found by conducting a word study. Taking the *Word Study Concordance and New Testament*, volume 1 you will turn to 2 Timothy 2:10. You'll notice that under the word "endure" is the number 5278.

Now take volume 2, the *Word Study Concordance*, and turn to word number 5278. The first thing that you'll see is a line of numbers it looks like this:

| 5278 | 17 | 853/979 | 4: 574 | 5259, 3306 |

The first number, 5278 is the Strong's word number. That means that this word when placed in alphabetical order with all of the other Greek words in the New Testament it is 5278th in line. You don't need to know any Greek it all to use his tool.

The second number is 17. This word occurs 17 times in the Greek New Testament. This number saves you a lot of trouble counting words that occur hundreds of times.

The third set of numbers, 853/979, tells us where to find this word in certain advanced Greek tools. We will not use this for our word study. The next set of numbers, 4:574 does the same thing. It refers to some scholarly Greek tools. If you wish more information about these numbers look in the word study concordance on pages viii-ix.

The final numbers, 5259, 3306, are the numbers of the root words from which this word is constructed.

Below the line of numbers or two words one written in Greek letters and the other written in English letters they look like this:

| υπομενω, hupomeno |

The first word is the Greek word we are studying, written in Greek letters. You do not need to be able to read this to do this study. If you'd like to know how this word is pronounced, look at the second word which transliterates the Greek word into English letters.

Under these words is a chart of the 17 occurrences of word number 5278 in the New Testament. Read the phrases in the chart. Notice that the English word that translates number 5278 is printed in italics. Did you notice anything unusual about these words in italics? You should have noticed that word number 5278 is translated by, *endureth, endure, tarried, behind, abode, patient, suffer,* and *take it patiently.*

The next step in your word study is to print the references for 5278 in a column down the left side of the page. You want to leave several lines of space between each reference. Your list will look something like this:

Mat 10:22

Mat 24:13

Mark 13:13

Luke: 2:43

Etc...

Next take your Bible and read each verse for number 5278, in context. As you read each verse ask yourself "what does this verse tell me about the meaning of number 5278?" You will want to ask yourself these questions: Who, What, When, Where,

Why, How, as applied to number 5278. In the right-hand column write down what you learn about number 5278 in that verse. Note that you are not writing down what you learn about the verse itself, but rather what you can learn about that particular word. You may need to read several verses before and after the reference to understand the context and be able to answer the questions about it. Be aware that some of the questions may not have an answer from the verse that you've read. For example a certain verse may not tell you when 5278 takes place.

The next step is to begin a word study summary chart. Here's where we correlate the results that we have discovered by examining each individual verse. In the word study summary we group our information under key question categories: Who, What, When, Where, Why, How. Take a look at the sample below for word number 5278.

Who	References
Disciples of Jesus	Mt 10:22; 24:13; Mk 13:13
Jesus	Lk 2:43
Silas and Timothy	Acts 17:14
Believers	Rom 12:12; 2 Tim 2:12
Jewish Believers	Heb 10:32
Paul	1 Tim 2:10

What	References
Hatred, Persecution	Mt 10:22; 24:13; Mk 13:13
Being in Jerusalem	Lk 2:43
The Uproar in Berea	Acts 17:14
Trials, Tribulations	Rom 12:12
All Things	2 Tim 2:12
Great Struggle, Confiscation	Heb 10:32

When	References
Just before the Second Coming	Mt 10:22; 24:13; Mk 13:13
At Passover, Jesus Was 12	Lk 2:43
Paul's Second Missionary Journey	Acts 17:14
Whenever We Have Trouble	Rom 12:12
While Exercising Spiritual Gifts	1 Cor 13:7
When Jews Became Christians	Heb 10:32
When Preaching the Gospel	2 Tim 2:10

Where	References
In Jerusalem	Lk 2:43
In Berea	Acts 17:14

Why	References
To Learn	Lk 2:43
To Do His Father's Business	Lk 2:43
To Continue Preaching the Gospel	Acts 17:14
To not be overcome by evil	Rom 12:12
For the Sake of the Elect	2 Tim 2:10

How	References
Patiently	Rom 12:12
While Praying Steadfastly	Rom 12:12
While Hoping and Believing	1 Cor 13:7
While Having Compassion	Heb 10:32

Now we have a summary of the usage of word number 5278. We know the: who, what, when, where, why, and how this word. It is now time to check the roots of the word.

Look up word 5259 in the concordance. Notice that the word occurs 230 times and is translated "of" "by" or "under." Look up word 3306. It occurs 120 times and seems to be consistently translated "abide" or "remain." Putting the roots together shows that 5278 seems to mean "abide by" or "remain under."

Conclusion

It is now time to formulate and test the conclusion. Based on the usage of the word throughout the New Testament supported by the root meaning of the word, it seems to mean to "remain under" a load. It carries the idea of "staying with it" even during a problem or when there is opposition. With that in mind test your conclusion by going back to each passage in which 5278 occurs. Does this trial definition fit with each verse? If there is a verse in which it does not fit ask yourself what is different and what to do to discover the definition that does fit that verse. Then try the new definition in all of the verses. If you cannot find a single definition that fits every verse you may have a word with more than one term meaning like the English word "post." You may need to recognize a set of two or more meanings for the word. In the case of word number 5278 the idea of "remaining under" seems to fit all the usages.

Now that you have done the work to discover on your own, strictly from the Bible, the definition of this word, you can now use a dictionary to check your work. You have discovered the meaning of the word all on your own simply using the Bible rather than running to the dictionary first. This is the essence of inductive Bible study. Your confidence will be greatly enhanced because you have looked up every occurrence of this word in the New Testament. You're basing your conclusion about this word on what the Bible says not on what some men told you.

Word Study Exercise

Do a study of the word "consolation" as found in Philemon 7. Follow the procedure that you have learned in the sample word study.

Chapter Five
APPLICATION

Application is the end result of our inductive Bible study. Observation answered the question, "What does it say?" Interpretation answered the question, "What does it mean?" Correlation answered the question, "What does the Word of God as a whole say about this subject?" And, application answers the question, "So what?" Application is the process of putting into practice that which we have learned from our inductive Bible study. James, the half-brother of Jesus, said, "But be doers of the word, and not hearers only..." James 1:22. It is a biblical imperative to study the Word of God for a resulting change.

It has been 10:53 in my office for several months now. I am reminded of this every time that I look up at the clock on my desk. I am pretty sure that the clock that I have was kicked out of the factory for eating batteries. So, one day I did "clock surgery" and removed the last battery that it will ever consume. It no longer eats batteries or keeps time, but it sure looks nice. It has all of the tools it needs to function, but it sits still, only looking good. In some sense, this characterizes the Christian who knows God's Word, but doesn't apply it. That Christian may have all of the tools that help Him understand the text, but he or she just sits still, only looking good to the passer-by.

Exegesis versus Application

With all of the classes that I have had on exegesis, I would have loved to have a class devoted to developing accurate, pointed applications. The foundation for becoming a fully functioning "clock" is set with proper Bible study, but unfortunately heresy isn't eliminated by proper study habits alone. Much heresy occurs through the development of applications. Haddon Robinson was once quoted as saying, "More heresy is preached in application than in Bible exegesis.[13]" This is alarming. This mistake creates a dysfunctional clock – a clock that doesn't tell true time. I think that I'd rather have a clock that doesn't work than one that is always off. So, how can we get started in developing accurate applications?

---

[13] Robinson, Haddon. *The Heresy of Application,* Preaching Today, 2007

Taking into consideration that proper inductive study has been done:

> 1. A person accurately understands the meaning of the message for the *original* audience
>
> 2. A person has taken into consideration the differences between the original situation and our situation
>
> 3. A person has discovered the particular principle (theological truth) communicated by that passage

There are a few guidelines that can help someone develop a pointed, true-to-the-text application.

Principles of Scriptural Application

> 1. Determine the original application(s) intended by the passage.
>
> 2. Evaluate the level of specificity of those applications to the original historical situations. If the original specific applications are transferable across time and space to other audiences, apply them in culturally appropriate ways.
>
> 3. If the original applications are not transferable, identify one or more broader cross-cultural principles that the specific elements of the text reflect.

4. Find appropriate applications for today that implement those principles.

Sometimes we apply the text in ways that might make the biblical writer say, "Wait a minute, that's the wrong use of what I said." This is the heresy of a good truth applied in the wrong way.

For example, I heard someone preach a sermon from Ruth on how to deal with in-laws. Now, it's true that in Ruth you have in-laws. The problem is, Ruth was not given to solve in-law problems. The sermon had a lot of practical advice, but it didn't come from the Scriptures.

Someone might ask, "What's the problem with preaching something true and useful, even if it's not the central thrust of your text or not what the writer had in mind?" When we preachers preach the Bible, we preach with biblical authority. We agree with Augustine: What the Bible says, God says. Therefore, we bring to bear on, say, this in-law problem, the full authority of God. The person hearing the sermon thinks, If I don't deal with my mother-in-law this way, I am disobedient to God. To me, that's a perversion of the Biblical text. You're saying what God doesn't say. One effect of this is you undermine what the Scripture truly means. Ultimately, people come to believe that anything with a biblical flavor is what God says.

The long-term effect is that we teach a mythology. Myth has an element of truth along with a great deal of fluff, and people tend to live in the fluff. They live with the implications of implications, and then they discover that what they thought God promised, he didn't promise.

In application we attempt to take the truth of the eternal God, which was given in a particular time and place and situation, and apply it to ourselves in the modern world. We who live in another time, another place, and a very different situation. That can be harder than it appears.

The Bible is specific—Paul writes letters to particular churches; the stories are specific. There are signals that may indicate we are confusing the questions. For instance, a text cannot mean what it has not meant. That is, when Paul wrote to people in his day, he expected them to understand what he meant. We cannot make that passage mean something today that it did not mean in principle in the ancient world. That's why we have to do diligent Bible study. We have to be honest with the text before we can bring it over to the contemporary world.

Constants in Application

Every passage has a vision of God, such as God as Creator or Sustainer or Holy. So find that first.

Second, ask, "What is the depravity factor? What in humanity rebels against that vision of God?"

These two questions are a helpful clue in application because God remains the same, and human depravity remains the same. Our depravity may look different, but it's the same pride, obstinacy, disobedience.

Bible genres have a direct effect on application as well. The most extensive Bible genre is story, people doing things. We have to ask, ―Why does the Bible give us so much narrative?" ―Why didn't God just come right out and say what he meant and not beat around the bush with stories?" God could have said, "Here are five principles about my will." But Hhe doesn't do that.

Therefore, it's dangerous to go into a narrative and say, "Here are three things we learn about the providence of God." That's not the way the biblical writers chose to handle it. If we believe the Bible to be the inspired Word of God, we have to consider the methods used to proclaim God's message.

The Holy Spirit has a direct role in the process of applying the text to the student's life. The Spirit answers to the Word. If we are faithful to the Scriptures, I give the Spirit of God something to work with.

Principles and Precepts

As we examine a passage of Scripture and discover a particular point of interest we should ask ourselves, ―Is this a principle or a precept?"

A **Principle** is a fundamental, primary, or general law or truth. It is a foundational doctrine, unhindered by time of geography. Example, ―Ice is cold." There has never been a time or place that this principle has not been true. Consider this statement, ―God is Holy." Principles are easy to apply, because they are constant.

A **precept** is a moral imperative given to a certain people for a certain task at a certain time. Consider the command given in Deuteronomy 14:8, ―Also the swine is unclean for you, because it has cloven hooves, yet does not chew the cud; you shall not eat their flesh or touch their dead carcasses." This command was given to the Children of Abraham prior to the death, burial and resurrection of Jesus. However, after the fulfillment of the Gospel we read, "But food does not commend us to God; for neither if we eat are we the better, nor if we do not eat are we the worse" 1 Corinthians 8:8.

Precepts are somewhat more difficult to apply than principles. When dealing with a precept we must consider some very important factors:

1. Who were the original recipients of the precept?
2. When was the precept taught?
3. Is there "direct correlation" between me and the original recipients?

Once we have grappled with these questions we will then know if and to what extent the precept applies to us.

Chapter Six
WRAP-UP

We have now considered introductory matters, learned to observe, dealt with the details of interpretation, practiced correlation, and learned to apply Scripture to our daily living. In this wrap-up section we will compare our study results with those of others in comparative study.

The Comparative Method

Now that we've completed our inductive study of Philemon it is time to benefit from the studies done by others. This is the time when we compare our results with commentators, authors of word studies, and others who have published results from their own studies of this book. Any number of tools may be used to compare our work with the work of others. A few kinds of these tools will be discussed here.

Commentaries

Believers think of commentaries immediately when we speak of comparative study. However, there are several different kinds of commentaries which have different kinds of value to the Bible student. It should be noted at this point that commentaries are primarily based on the author's interpretation of Scripture. With this in mind it should be understood that there are conservative commentaries, liberal commentaries, good commentaries and bad commentaries.

Exegetical commentaries are commentaries based on the original languages of the Bible. They treat technical issues of the Greek and Hebrew. But be warned, some exegetical commentaries are written by unbelievers who have an interest in scholarly Greek and Hebrew.

Technical commentaries are usually based on the English text but give some attention to Greek or Hebrew words and syntax. They are easier to use than exegetical commentaries for the English bound student.

Analytical commentaries are usually based on the English text and emphasize the argument of the book of the Bible. They tend to present an outline of the book and show how that outline supports the theme of the book as they see it.

Devotional commentaries are based on the English text and emphasize application. Most of the commentaries in this group do not go verse by verse but tend to comment on themes the author wishes to emphasize.

This classification system has limited value because commentaries do not usually declare what kind they are. Their dust-jackets sometimes have comments which will provide clues for observant readers. Sometimes the categories I have mentioned overlap so that the distinctions may not be clear.

There is a group of books that can help students to evaluate commentaries. These are annotated bibliographies in which the author of the bibliography evaluate different books and makes recommendations. The most important thing about these bibliographies is to know the viewpoint of the bibliographer. His recommendations will generally reflect his own personal position.

There are a number of books and sets of books which present word studies. These can be utilized to evaluate your word study results. Of these this author prefers A.T. Robertson's *Word Studies in the Greek New Testament.*

In all comparative study is good for learning what others believe, but don't be too quick to assume that they are correct and that you are wrong. However, allow this to be an opportunity to look for specific flaws in your process or conclusions. Be aware that when a discrepancy is discovered between your study and the study of others that they may have different presuppositions or other hermeneutical standards than you do. Do not automatically rush to their position.

Theology books can be used to evaluate the results of your study, particularly in doctrinal areas. It is good to discover theology books that share your theological position and hermeneutics and which have Scripture as well as topical indexes. In that way they can be used for reference books by simply looking for your particular passage in the Scripture index.

The Mechanics of Comparative Study

The mechanics of comparative study are simple indeed. When you have completed your personal inductive study, jot down any conclusions you would like to verify. Then find the appropriate books you can use to compare other authors results with your own. As mentioned above, don't be too quick to change your view when there is a disagreement. Look at this as an opportunity to conduct further study to either refute or confirm your conclusion. Look for sound logic that compels you to re-examine your position.

You have now conducted an inductive Bible study. You have available to you the skills and tools necessary to be able to study Scripture on your own. Never again will you find yourself dependent upon other people to tell you what to believe. However, as good as it is that you have these tools, and skills, we are still commanded in Scripture to fellowship together Heb 10:25, and to learn from others who have more knowledge than ourselves. It is the prayer of this author that this study has enhanced your ability to interact with God's word, but that it not be misused in order to puff up the reader. Let each of us be consistent, humble, diligent students of God's Word.

I pray that God will certainly enrich your walk with him and that ~~the~~ eyes of your understanding being enlightened; that you may know what is the hope of His calling, what are the riches of the glory of His inheritance in the saints…"

Selected Bibliography

Aland, Kurt. *The Greek New Testament with Dictionary.* Edmonds: United Bible Society 1966

Anders, Max. *New Christian's Handbook.* Nashville: Nelson 1999

Anderson, Ken. *Where to Find it in the Bible.* Nashville: Nelson 1996

Axelrod, Rise B. and Charles R. Cooper. *The St. Martin's Guide to Writing.* Boston: Bedford 2001

Braga, James. *How to Study the Bible.* Portland: Multnomah 1982

Brown, Francis and et al. *The Brown-Driver-Briggs Hebrew and English Lexicon.* Peabody: Hendrickson 1999

Bryant, T. Alton - Ed. *Compact Bible Dictionary.* Grand Rapids: Regency 1967

Bullinger, E. W. *Figures of Speech Used in the Bible.* Grand Rapids: Baker 1968

Bullock, C. Hassell. *An Introduction to the Old Testament Prophetic Books.* Chicago: Moody 1986

Comfort, Philip Wesley - Ed. *The Origin of the Bible.* Wheaton: Tyndale

Cox, Steven. *Essentials of New Testament Greek - A Student's Guide.* Broadman & Holman

Dana, H. E. and Julius R. Mantey. *A Manual Grammar of the Greek New Testament.* Upper Saddle River: Prentice Hall 1927

Dueck, Alvin C. *Between Jerusalem & Athens.* Grand Rapids: Baker 1995

Eade, Alfred Thompson. *The Expanded Panorama Bible Study Course.* Grand Rapids: Revell 1961

Edersheim, Alfred. *Bible History - Old Testament.* Peabody: Hendrickson 1995

Elliger, K. *Biblia Hebraica – Stuttgartensia.* Deutsche Biblegesellschaft 1969

Elwell, Walter A. *Evangelical Dictionary of Theology.* Cumbria: Baker 1984

Enns, Paul. *The Moody Handbook of Theology.* Chicago: Moody 1989

Farstad, Arthur. *The NKJV Greek English Interlinear New Testament.* Nashville: Nelson 1994

Geisler, Norman L. *A General Introduction to the Bible.* Chicago: Moody 1968

Geisler, Norman L. and William E. Nix. *From God to Us.* Chicago: Moody 1974

Grassmick, John D. *Principles and Practice of Greek Exegesis* Dallas: Dallas Theological Seminary 1974

Greenberg, Moshe. *Introduction to Hebrew.* Englewood Cliffs: Prentice Hall 1965

Halley, Henry H. *Halley's Bible Handbook.* Grand Rapids: Zondervan 1927

Hastings, James - Ed. *Hastings' Dictionary of the Bible.* New York: Hendrickson 1909

Hester, H. I. *The Heart of Hebrew History.* Nashville: Broadman 1962

Hodges, C. Zane. *The Greek New Testament according to the Majority Text.* Nashville: Nelson 1985

House, H. Wayne - Ed. *Chronological and Background Charts of the New Testament.* Grand Rapids: Zondervan 1981

Jensen, Irving L. *Jensen's Survey of the New Testament.* Chicago: Moody 1981

Jensen, Irving L. *Jensen's Survey of the Old Testament.* Chicago: Moody 1978

Kelley, Page H. *Biblical Hebrew.* Grand Rapids: Eerdmans 1992

Kent, Homer A. *Jerusalem to Rome Studies in Acts.* Grand Rapids: Baker 1972

Kubo, Sakae. *A Reader's Greek-English Lexicon of the New Testament.* Zondervan

Lightfoot, J. B. *Biblical Essays.* Hendrickson 1893

McDonald, Lee M. *The Formation of the Christian Biblical Canon.* Peabody: 1995

Perschbacher, Wesley J. *The New Analytical Greek Lexicon.* Peabody: Hendrickson 1990

Radmacher, Earl and et al - Eds. *New Illustrated Bible Commentary.* Nashville: Nelson 1999

Ramm, Bernard. *Protestant Biblical Interpretation.* Grand Rapids: Baker 1970

Robertson, Archibald. *Word Pictures in the New Testament Set 1 – 6.* Broadman

Ryken, Leland. *How to Read the Bible as Literature.* Grand Rapids: Academic Books 1984

Strong, James. *The New Strong's Exhaustive Concordance of the Bible.* Nashville: Nelson 1964

Summers, Ray. *Essentials of New Testament Greek.* Nashville: Broadman & Holman 1995

Turabian, Kate L. *A Manual for Writers of Term Papers, Theses, and Dissertations (Sixth edition).* Chicago: the University of Chicago 1996

Unger, Merrill F. *The New Unger's Bible Dictionary.* Moody

Vine, W. E. *Vine's Complete Expository Dictionary of Old & New Testament Words.* Nashville: Nelson 1984

Virkler, Henry. *Hermeneutics.* Grand Rapids: Baker 1981

Wallace, Daniel B. *Greek Grammar Beyond the Basics.* Grand Rapids: Zondervan 1996

Wallace, Daniel B. *The Basics of New Testament Syntax.* Grand Rapids: Zondervan 2000

Walvoord, John F. and Roy B. Zuck. *The Bible Knowledge Commentary (New Testament).* Colorado Springs: Victor 1983

Wassman, Rose and Anne Paye. *A Reader's Handbook.* Glenview: Scott, Foresman and Company 1985

Wiersbe, Warren W. *The Bible Exposition Commentary.* Colorado Springs: Victor 1989

Wigram, George V. and Ralph D. Winter. *The Word Study New Testament and Concordance.* Wheaton: Wheaton 1972

Wilkinson, Bruce and Kenneth Boa. *Talk thru the Bible.* Nashville: Nelson 1983

Wilkinson, Bruce. *Talk thru Bible Personalities.* Nashville: Walk Thru the Bible 1983

Wood, Leon J. *A Survey of Israel's History.* Grand Rapids: Zondervan 1970

Wood, Leon J. *The Prophets of Israel.* Grand Rapids: Baker

Zodhiates, Spiros. *The Complete Word Study Dictionary of the New Testament.* Chattanooga: AMG Publishers 1992

Zuck, Roy B. - Ed. *A Biblical Theology of the New Testament.* Chicago: Moody 1994

Zuck, Roy B. - Ed. *A Biblical Theology of the Old Testament.* Chicago: Moody 1991

Zuck, Roy B. *Basic Bible Interpretation.* Colorado Springs: Victor 1991

Zuck, Roy B. *The Bible Knowledge Commentary 2 Vol. Set.* Colorado Springs: Victor 1983

Also Available:

Salvation:
God's Greatest Miracle
Clay A. Kahler Ph.D.

God, the creator and sustainer of the universe, lovingly and intentionally provided all that is needed for the reconciliation of man to Himself, through Jesus Christ. In this book you will learn what God's plan of salvation is and how to receive it for yourself. Paul the apostle tells us that peace, joy, and hope are ours for the taking, through the gospel.

Dr. Kahler approaches this most important biblical doctrine in his typical no-nonsense, plain-talking style. It is a must-read for all who are saved and for those who are struggling with the idea of salvation.

ISBN: 1556355246

Available from Christian bookstores and online book sellers nationwide.

Simple Theology:
Theology for the Rest of Us
Clay A. Kahler Ph.D.

This survey of theology is suited for every believer, regardless of previous knowledge or spiritual maturity. Dr. Kahler presents theological truths in a way that is easy to understand and will spur the reader on to further study.

ISBN: 1579108873

Available from Christian bookstores and online book sellers nationwide.

Against Protestant Popes:
An Exegetical Study of 1 Peter 5:1-4 (Paperback)
Clay A. Kahler Ph.D.

A BIBLICAL LOOK at God's awesome call to be a shepherd to His flock. This exegetical look at Peter's admonition to "fellow Shepherds" will cause those in ministry to look very hard at their own model of ministry. Packed full of Biblical insights, this is a must read for all of those in or considering the ministry.

ISBN: 1597521493

Available from Christian bookstores and online book sellers nationwide.

Torn Asunder:
A Biblical Look at Divorce and Remarriage (Paperback)
Dr. Clay A. Kahler

In *Torn Asunder: A Biblical Look at Divorce and Remarriage* Dr. Kahler tackles one of today's most controversial topics. When discussing divorce and remarriage passions run deep. That is why this book is so important. Dr. Kahler leads the reader through a Biblical exploration seeking God's instruction, dispelling myths and tackling tradition. No matter your feelings on the subject, this book will help you discover God's heart concerning those who have been hurt and those currently suffering.

ISBN: 1597528072

Available from Christian bookstores and online book sellers nationwide.

www.ingramcontent.com/pod-product-compliance
Lightning Source LLC
Chambersburg PA
CBHW071515150426
43191CB00009B/1531